MW01093982

Dedicated in loving memory
to Howard Ansley Peacock, Jr.,
who, beyond a well tuned guitar and a properly
chilled beer, loved few things more than a
good race.

The Commode Side Guide To
Stock Car Racing History

First Things First

The first stock car competitions that are recognizable ancestors of today's super speedway races, though rarely sanctioned and loosely organized, began to appear in the nineteen thirties. However, prior to this, a myriad of events occurred, the obvious and subtle effects of which are still felt today.

Certainly, the invention of the automobile ranks highest among these. In Europe, two Germans, Gottlieb Daimler and Karl Benz, working independently,had developed their first crude automobiles by 1885. It is generally agreed that the first American automobile was the creation of J. Frank Duryea of Springfield, Massachusetts. Duryea did not introduce his machine, however, until 1893.

The following year, 1894, would witness what was truly a water shed event in the annals of automobile racing. The Paris-Rouen race was staged on July 22. Actually billed as a reliability trial, the contest was sponsored by a newspaper called "Le Petit Journal" and followed a course that ran approximately seventy-eight miles. The starting point was the Boulevard Maillot, and while one hundred and two contestants had entered, only twenty-one managed to appear at the start. After stopping for lunch and dodging the spectators who felt compelled to run amongst the moving cars, the first vehicle to the finish was a steam powered wagon with a trailer attached. However, because it took more than one person to operate and burned an exorbitant amount of coal, it was disqualified. As a result, two of the thirteen gas powered cars that had finished, a Panhard & Levassor and a Peugeot, split the first place prize of 12,000 francs.

While Americans lagged significantly behind Europeans in the development of the automobile, they were not so far behind the curve when it came to racing. In 1895 H.H.Kohlsaat decided to sponsor a race through his newspaper, the "Chicago Times-Herald". The contest was scheduled for November 2. However,when it became clear that few, if any, of the nearly one hundred entries would be ready in time, the race was postponed until Thanksgiving Day, November 28. In lieu of the race, however, a round trip exhibition to Waukegan and back was held on the original date. Only two vehicles, a Mueller-Benz and a Duryea, participated. Due to numerous mechanical difficulties the Duryea was unable to finish and the Mueller-Benz, for a time of eight hours and forty-four minutes, was awarded a five hundred dollar prize.

When Thanksgiving, the day of the actual race arrived, conditions were abhorrent. Temperatures were never above freezing, winds neared sixty miles per hour, and up to a foot of snow and ice was on the ground. Only six vehicles made it to the start: three Benz powered machines, two electrics, and the Duryea. J. Frank Duryea, in his own machine, was the first to start at 8:55 a.m., while the Mueller-Benz, having been tardy, was the last to depart at 10:06 a.m.

The course this time was from Chicago to Evanston and back. Despite the weather, large crowds lined most of the route. The Duryea led the entire race and, despite a ten minute delay due to a wrong turn, was the first car to return to the finish line at Jackson Park in Chicago. In the ten hours and fifty-three minutes that it took Duryea to complete the course most of the crowds had disappeared. Oscar Mueller brought the Mueller-Benz to the finish for second place. With it's time adjusted for the late start the Mueller-Benz was twenty-four minutes off the pace. J. Frank Duryea had won the first automobile race in America with an average speed of 6.66 miles per hour.

Duryea also won America's second automobile race on May 30,1896. This race was sponsored by "Cosmopolitan" magazine and ran from New York City to Ardsley Country Club in Irvington, New York. Duryea, the only finisher, completed the thirty miles in seven hours and thirteen minutes and was awarded three thousand dollars. In September of the same year the first of countless dirt track races in the United States was held. Actually, it was a series of one mile races run at the Rhode Island State Fair at Narragansett Park. The eventual winner was an electric car driven by A.L. Riker and C.H.Whiting.

Perhaps the most significant event of this era, however, was the development of Henry Ford's first prototype in 1896. The machine featured wire bicycle-type wheels, a three to four horsepower engine, two forward gears, no reverse, and an electric doorbell for a horn. It was successfully tested in a light rain on a June morning at about two a.m. However, before Ford could test drive his contraption, he had to take an ax to the doorway of the shed where he had built it because the machine was too big to go through. It would not be long before Ford would enter into the world of racing. In the years after his first test run Ford was obsessed with the idea of mass producing his machine. However, his attempts to establish an automobile company were all aborted.

In 1901 Ford decided to build a racing car. A crew of five was employed to build the vehicle with the aim of entering a race at Grosse Pointe Race Track near Detroit. Grosse Pointe was a horse track which had been modified with banked turns to accommodate automobiles. The twenty-five mile race took place on October 10 and featured an under card of steam and electric racers. Ford's car boasted what may have been the first ever spark plugs and could generate twenty-six horsepower. However, his competitor, Alexander Winton, manned a machine capable of seventy horsepower. Winton had won at Grosse Pointe before as well as other tracks. He also had set speed and endurance marks and was perhaps the first "star" of American racing. Both drivers had a henchman hanging off the side of the car to act as ballast. When the race began Winton quickly pulled away, showing that he had superior driving skills as well as a superior racer. However, Ford was able to trim the lead as he slowly got the feel of the track. Then Winton's machine began to overheat. Attempts to cool it by pouring oil on it proved futile. Ford moved ahead on the eighth lap and beat Winton to the finish with an average speed of about forty-two miles per hour. He was awarded a cut glass bowl amidst the cheers of a jubilant crowd.

Machines were quickly becoming capable of speeds that no city streets in Europe or America could accommodate. One of the places that racers turned to was a stretch of sand in Florida between Ormond Beach and Daytona Beach. We find Alexander Winton here again, pitted against Ranson E. Olds, in 1902. It was reported that the Winton Bullet and the Oldsmobile Pirate had attained identical speeds of 50 miles per hour. Although earlier tests had been held on beaches in the Northeast, the wide beach and hard sand at Daytona proved so favorable to drivers that it would soon earn the moniker "The Birthplace of Speed".

William K. Vanderbilt, Jr., who donated the Vanderbilt Cup to the recently formed AAA and who held the land speed record on several occasions, came to Daytona in 1903. Henry Ford followed in 1904. On January 12 Ford had set a speed record of 91.37 mph on frozen Lake St. Clair. Fifteen days later he arrived at Daytona just in time to see Vanderbilt break his record. Later that same season Vanderbilt became the first man to break the 100 mph barrier. He received no credit for the record, however, since he had not been officially timed.

Ormond-Daytona soon attracted the greatest drivers from both Europe and America, and the beach was the scene of many momentous events. In 1906 Fred Marriott, driving a Stanley Steamer Rocket, set a record of 127.66 mph which would stand for four years. The following year he crashed at approximately 150 mph and was thrown into the water. Though Marriott survived, it was the last run for a Stanley Steamer. Marriott's record stood until 1910 when Barney Oldfield pushed a 200 horsepower Blitzen-Benz to a speed of 131.72 mph.

A milestone of inestimable importance occurred in 1908.This was the year Henry Ford introduced his Model T. Dozens of companies had produced cars for years prior to this. However, to produce a vehicle that was efficient, reliable, and most importantly, affordable to the working man, had been Ford's particular ambition. With the Model T, the prototypical stock car, he succeeded. The first T rolled off the assembly line in October 1908, and carried a price tag of $850. The next year a Model T was the winner of a New York to Seattle race, beating out several foreign models which were priced as much as four times as the low end Fords. The Model T proved so dependable that 15 million of basically the same type were produced, affording millions of Americans their introduction to the automotive world.

The template for NASCAR's modern super speedways was begun in 1908, the same year the Model T was introduced. This was more than fifty years before Daytona and more than forty years before Darlington. The Indianapolis Motor Speedway was the brainchild of Carl Fischer, a barnstormer turned businessman. His partners in 1908 were James Allison, Arthur Newby, and Frank Wheeler. Initial financing for the project was $75,000.

With a surface of crushed stone and tar, the 2.5 mile rectangle was complete in 1909. However, the first competition held there in June was a balloon race. In August 1909 the first automobile race was held. Accidents were so prevalent it was determined that a new surface was necessary. The solution the owners came up with was to pave the speedway with 3.2 million bricks. Though the bricks were replaced with tarmac during the 1930's and asphalt in 1961,the nickname "Brickyard" has remained. 1911 witnessed the introduction of another standard later adopted by NASCAR: the 500 mile race. Ray Harroun , who had several cross country records and won numerous AAA sanctioned races, came out of retirement just for this inaugural race and was rewarded with a victory. The series has continued until the present, interrupted only by the two World Wars.

On March 29, 1927, Henry Segrave made a record run at Daytona in a Sunbeam racer. This was a 1000 horsepower, twin engined monster of a machine. In it, Segrave broke the 200 mph mark with a speed of 203.79 mph. For his efforts Segrave was knighted. On March 7,1935, Sir Malcolm

Campbell drove his Bluebird II to a mark of 276.82 mph. In September of the same year he took the same car to the Bonneville Salt Flats in Utah and broke the 300 mph mark. This signaled the end of land speed record runs at Daytona. However, in a not so indirect way, it marked the beginning of Daytona's history as a mecca of stock car racing

A final pre-Depression event cannot be overlooked. This is the one-two punch of the Eighteenth Amendment and the Volstead Act,which brought America Prohibition in 1919. Though President Hoover would later commend Prohibition as a "noble experiment", it was also a failed experiment almost from it's very beginning.

Almost immediately liquor began flowing across the Canadian and Mexican borders. In Los Angeles, Miami, and New York booze was smuggled aboard incoming vessels. In Chicago and New York the thousands of speakeasies were supplied by organized crime syndicates. The most notorious of these was run by Chicago's infamous Al Capone. In these and other Northern cities,large indoor distilling operations were not unusual. Prohibition was probably of least concern to the drinkers in the Southeast. Moonshiners had been distilling illicit liquor, in Appalachia and other remote regions, quite literally for centuries. What Prohibition brought was a demand in cities like Nashville,Birmingham,Atlanta,Charlotte, and Washington, , D.C., that had not existed before. The term "bootlegger" had been used to describe one who smuggled whiskey for many years. However,in the era of temperance, the men who would haul the moonshiner's wares to the big cities via automobile, were an entirely new breed. From their ranks would rise some of the greatest of the early stock car racers.

Many early racing series were centered around certain communities which found it profitable to turn their streets over to speed jockeys once a year. Two famous examples are Elgin, Illinois and Savannah, Georgia, both of which staged successful road races for several years. A city which did not enjoy so much success was Corona, California, a farming community fifty miles east of Los Angeles. With a 2.77 mile dirt avenue encircling the city, Corona seemed destined to host an automobile race. Under the pretense of commemorating California's admission to the union, the city fathers decided to do just that on September 9,1913. The AAA sanctioned race drew stars such as Ralph DePalma and Barney Oldfield, and a crowd of 100,000. As a warm up for the open wheeled racers, a stock car race was run. In this very early example the top three finishers were a Buick, an REO, and a Studebaker.

Through the 1920's and into the into the '30's, the stock cars of the day were regular participants in three types of competitions. These were endurance runs, straightaway runs at Daytona, and the Pikes Peak Hill Climb. Along with Ford and Chrysler, some of the makes represented were Essex, Auburn, and Studebaker.

Even more so than Indianapolis, the paradigm for today's Sprint Cup super speedways was the wooden board tracks which enjoyed enormous popularity in the 1920's. These behemoths were largely the brainchild of Fred Moscoviks, a one time engineer for Daimler. His idea was to copy the steep banks of a bicycle velodrome. Moscoviks persuaded a group of California businessmen to build two tracks under the supervision of Jack Prince, an English bicycle champion. These first two tracks were Playa Del Ray and Elmhurst, both in California. Neither would last for long, but they foreshadowed a board track boom.

By the summer of 1927 stock car races were beginning to take their modern form. Some good examples are races which were run in the northeast portion of the country. On July 4, an Indy car race was run at Rockingham Speedway, a one and a quarter mile board track in Salem, New Hampshire. As a preliminary, a 100 mile stock car race was run. Open wheeled ace Frank Lockhart led the field of six for most of the distance, but two blowouts cost him first place. That distinction went to Waite Morton, while Ralph Hepburn finished third.

On Labor Day, 1927, two stock car races were run at Atlantic City Speedway, a one and a half mile board track in Amatol, New Jersey. The main event was a 150 mile race for six and eight cylinder cars. Gil Anderson of Indianapolis led almost the entire race, but engine trouble forced him to a third place finish. The winner was Tom Rooney, also of Indianapolis, with a speed of 96.30 mph. L.L. Corum was second and Ralph Hepburn was fourth. Hepburn had won a warm up race for six cylinder cars earlier in the day. His speed in that 75 mile event was 85.94 mph. A crowd of 75,000 was on hand for both events.

Many of the AAA stars of the board track era sometimes competed in stock car events. This was the case on August 26, 1933 near Chicago, when a series of races was run on the historic Elgin road course. Part of the bill was a 203 mile stock car race. On a surface of concrete, bitumen, and gravel, Fred Frame drove a Ford to a first place finish with a speed of 80.22 mph. As was the custom at the time, Frame's mechanic, Eddie Malin, sat in the passenger seat. The field consisted of fifteen cars, but after the first eight crossed the finish line the race was halted. After Frame the top finishers were Lou Moore of Los Angeles, Jack Petticord of Chicago, Eugene Haustein of Detroit, Frank Briskow of Milwaukee, Wilbur Shaw of Detroit, Shorty Cantlon of Detroit, and "Wild Bill" Cummings of Indianapolis.

Another similar race was held on February 18,1934 at Los Angeles Municipal Airport. The 250 mile race over a 1.9 mile road course attracted the likes of Chet Gardner, Lou Meyer, and Rex Mays. However, the victor was a relative unknown, Al Gordon of Long Beach, California. Before a crowd of 50,000, Gordon had averaged 60.33 mph.

A few weeks later, on April 23, a big name did claim the checkered flag. In a 151 mile race on the road course at Ascot, the winner was Lou Meyer in a Ford. His average speed had been 51.33 mph.

No date can be singled out as the origin of stock car racing. However, one that comes tantalizingly close is March 8,1936.

As Franklin D. Roosevelt ushered in his New Deal, the chamber of commerce of Daytona Beach found themselves in search of a new deal of their own.

The international time trials at Daytona had begun to attract crowds so sizable that grandstands had been constructed to accommodate them. It was partially because of the safety hazard presented by the crowds that the trials were moved to the Bonneville Salt Flats in Utah. Sir Malcolm Campbell's record breaking run in 1935 would prove to be one of the last.

However, while the crowds were a bane to the drivers, they were a godsend to the local businesses. To keep the people and the dollars flowing in, a scheme was devised whereby the city council would sponsor a stock car race on the beach. Even the most prescient among them could not have foreseen what the event would one day become.

The course laid out was 3.2 miles long. It utilized a 1.5 mile section of the beach where speed trials had been held. After racing north on the beach, cars would make a sharp left hand turn onto highway A1A and head south. After another mile and a half on asphalt a second left hand turn would return the cars to the beach to complete the oval course.

The turn at the north end of the "track" was located just at the center of town,and was the scene of numerous accidents during practice prior to the race. In one of these Bobby Sall, of Paterson, New Jersey, sustained life threatening injuries when he overturned a car owned by Rudy Adams. Sall recovered, but on race day, in anticipation of more mayhem, the highest concentration of spectators was at this turn.

Twenty-seven men qualified seven different makes of cars to

get their chance at the 5,000 dollars in prize money. Paving the way many Northerners would follow after the war, Landon Quinby and Sam Collier came all the way from New York. Collier was the slowest qualifier, at 58.60 mph, but because the field would be inverted, started first. An Auburn, driven by"Wild Bill"Cummings, was credited with the fastest speed of 70.39 mph. As a former Indy champion Cummings helped to garner attention from the press.

When race day arrived a seven mile road to the nearest hospital was closed to all traffic except emergency vehicles. The twenty-seven machines, stripped of bumpers and headlights, lined up in inverted order at one p.m. Not only was the field inverted, but the starts were staggered, so that Bill Cummings started a full thirty minutes behind Sam Collier.

The course proved too tough to tame, however. A number of cars became stuck or overturned in the notorious north turn. Also, the tide began to come in, threatening spectators and their cars. All this resulted in the race being halted at around two hundred miles, though it had been scheduled for two hundred and fifty.

The high attrition rate and the staggered start made it difficult to determine the winner for several days. Eventually, Milt Marion was declared the first place finisher. He had ridden to victory in a Ford V-8, as had all of the top five. It was the fifth place finisher, above all others, for whom posterity would reserve a place. His name was Bill France.

In actuality, the success that William Henry Getty France would achieve after his fifth place finish is attributable less to Providence and more to his own foresight and determination.

France's odyssey had begun humbly enough, in Horsepasture, Virginia, on September 26, 1909. He was raised in the Washington, D.C. area where he attended Central High School. High school lasted only two years, however, before France dropped out and found a job as a mechanic.

During this period France began to race in the Maryland area at venues such as the board track at Laurel and the dirt track at Pikesville. Before he had his own car his father would gladly loan him the family's Model T, unaware that young Bill was racing it in competitions where speeds could exceed one hundred miles per hour. He also raced up and down the East coast, occasionally as far away as the board tracks at Altoona, Pennsylvania and Atlantic City.

The only thing for which France felt the same attraction he felt for cars and racing was Annie Bledsoe, a nurse from Nathan's Creek, North Carolina. They were married in June 1931, and soon were blessed with the addition of William, Jr., whom they called Billy.

In 1934 France made a fateful decision:he would move his young family South. He has stated that he resolved to do so using this rationale:If he was going to struggle by on a mechanic's wages in a depressed economy, he may as well do it in a balmier climate. The sunshine state, Florida, seemed to fit the bill.

The legend persists that they settled in Daytona because that is where the family car gave up the ghost. However,France insisted that had his car broken down, he merely would have repaired it and been on his way. He contended that their arrival in the fall of 1934 was entirely intentional, he being lured in part by the prospect of seeing the speed trials.

France would not be disappointed in that regard. In March 1935 he was on hand to see Malcolm Campbell's record setting run in his Bluebird II. Shortly afterward he was able to land a mechanic's job at Sax Lloyd's Buick-Pontiac-Cadillac. The next year, France found himself behind the wheel in the inaugural beach race, bringing home $500 for his fifth place effort.

He also competed in the 1937 edition of the beach race. This one was sponsored by the Elk's Club because the Camber of Commerce claimed that the city lost $22,000 on the first race. Another change was that the race was shortened to one hundred miles. What remained the same was Bill's failure to find the winner's circle. That honor went to Tommy Elmore, once again in a V-8 Ford. Bill did get to claim the Ford that was the envy of everyone at the local dirt tracks that year. It was a '37 coupe, and proudly emblazoned on it's side was the name of Bill's sponsor:Charlie's Grill and Cocktail Bar.

When 1938 rolled around the Chamber of Commerce, leery of losing more money, asked Bill for ideas on promoting the beach race. He thought a nearby hotel owner, Ralph Hankinson, who also promoted races, might be the solution. Unfortunately,when France placed a collect call to pitch the idea to him, Hankinson refused to accept the charges.

Apparently,larger forces were at work, because at this point destiny intervened. It did so in the person of Charlie Reese, Bill's sponsor and owner of Charlie's Grill and Cocktail Bar. Reese proposed that if Bill would handle the promotional details, he would put up the necessary money, and they would split the profits. There were no profits to split, however,despite the fact that 5000 tickets were sold at a cost of fifty cents each.

France was also on hand later in 1938 for what was billed as the "world's championship stock car race". This 150 mile event was stage at Lakewood Speedway, a one mile dirt oval in Atlanta, Georgia. The track had been so christened because there was a small lake in it's center. Built originally as a two mile horse track in 1890, it was reconfigured to one mile in 1915, using forced convict labor. The area around it became known as the Southeastern Fairgrounds, and featured exhibition halls and restaurants. A roller coaster was added to all of this the following year. Horse and motorcycle competitions were the first races there. Later, the open cockpit cars that raced at Indianapolis, along with their big name drivers, made frequent appearances.

With the 1938 stock car race on Armistice Day, qualifying heats were held on the preceding Sunday and Thursday. Twelve drivers qualified on each day to comprise a field of twenty-four. In addition to Bill France, some of the best known stock car racers of the day were present. Dan Murphy , Smoky Purser, and Henri Guerand helped France represent Daytona Beach. Harley Taylor, Roy Hall, Red Singleton, and Red Byron were among the flock of drivers which operated out of Atlanta. Perhaps the most famous entrant was Joie Chitwood. He had been born George Rice Chitwood on April 14, 1912 in Deneison, Texas. In a career which began in 1935 in Anthony, Kansas, Chitwood would be AAA Dirt Track Champion, Central States Racing Association Champion, and Oklahoma State Stock Car Champion. He would also compete in seven

Indianapolis 500's, finishing fifth on three separate occasions. He had adapted the name "Joie" when a reporter mistakenly identified him as such. Also, because of his Cherokee ancestry, reporters of the day would invariably place "Chief" in front of his name.

The claim that this was the "world's championship" was not without merit. This is due to the fact that the Central States Auto Racing Association, the International Stock Car Racing Association, the Motor Internationale, the Atlantic States Racing Association, and the Gulf States Auto Association all sanctioned the race. Despite all the big name participants the winner was essentially a rookie. Twenty-one year old Lloyd Seay, a native of Dawsonville,Georgia, was declared the victor when the race was halted after 135 miles due to darkness. He had raced his way through the field several times after suffering two flat tires. Despite the impressive array of sanctioning bodies, the scoring became so confused that the prize money for second through sixth place had to be pooled and split evenly. The rest of the top finishers were Joie Chitwood, Dan Murphy, Roy Hall,Pete Craig, and Bill France. It would be this kind of mayhem which would later inspire France to form NASCAR. This race was such a financial success that two more races were organized in the waning months of 1938. One was at Macon, Georgia and the second was again at Lakewood. The winner of both these events was an Ohioan, Larry Beckett.

A poor showing in '38 did not deter Bill France and Charlie Reese from returning as promoters of the 1939 Daytona beach race. Again they sold 5000 tickets, this time at one dollar a piece, with a much better result. A profit of $2000 was realized,but more importantly,Bill France was set on the course that would lead him to greatness. From this point forward his inestimable influence on stock car racing would be effected not from behind the wheel, but from behind his desk.

Again in 1939, Lakewood Speedway would host what was billed as a national championship stock car race. Instead of Armistice Day it was held on Labor Day,September 4. It was sponsored by the Southeastern Fair Association, whose president was Mike Benton. Benton proudly announced that the application of a special oil would control the dust for which Lakewood was notorious. The track also boasted a brand new scoreboard for the event.

That scoreboard would show Red Singleton of Atlanta on the pole. The field also featured Fontello 'Fonty' Flock and Bob Flock, starting sixth and twelfth, respectively. Fonty and Bob were two of a legendary trio of racing brothers who had emigrated from Fort Payne, Alabama to Atlanta. Among the cars featured that day were eight Ford Coaches, seven Ford Coupes, two Ford Roadsters,one Ford Sedan, one Ford four-door,and one Ford Tudor. The lone non-Ford was a Graham South Carolina, driven by Bob Baker of Canton,Ohio.

Not surprisingly, the top eight finishers were Fords. The winner was Roy Hall, followed by Jap Brogdon, Bob Flock, Ben Tatum, Jr., Buddy Johnston, J.L.Simpson, and Bob Reid. Hall received $350 as a first place prize. While he had been warmly received in the winner's circle,he was not welcome on the streets of Atlanta,as his license had been recently revoked. However,Hall's relationship with the local constabulary was not entirely unpleasant. Once,a federal revenue agent supposedly became involved in a chase with a suspected liquor car near the Georgia town of Tate. While attempting to duplicate one of the suspects turns,he wrecked his car and sustained rather serious injuries. While in the hospital he received a bouquet of flowers,which he later learned had come compliments of his driving adversary,Roy Hall.

In 1939 races were also held at Salisbury, North Carolina and Spartanburg,South Carolina. These were promoted by Joe Littlejohn, who had previously staged Indy type and motorcycle races at these venues.

Racing activity at this time was not confined to the South.1939 also saw a stock car race at Langhorne Speedway. Langhorne was a one mile dirt track in Bucks County, Pennsylvania. It was built by a group calling itself the National Motor Racing Association. The Association's President was Bill Strickler and it's Secretary was Al Jacobs. The project began with the purchase of 89 acres on U.S. Route 1, at a cost of $27,000.

However,the area proved to be rife with springs, making con-struction difficult. This necessitated bringing in new investors. At a meeting with these new investors it was decided that the track would have a circular shape. Under the name New Philadelphia Speedway, opening day was set for May 31,1926. However, rain delayed the first race until June 12.

In 1928-29 attendance at the track dropped, so much so that it nearly closed. It was then taken over by Ralph Hankinson, the same gentleman who would later refuse Bill France's collect call. Hankinson brought in some of the big names of the day, including Bill Cummings, Fred Frame, and Ralph DePalma. On May 16,1937, Langhorne was the scene of a terrible accident. An overflow crowd produced problems as rowdy spectators kept trying to run across the track, and the inevitable came to pass. Two boys ran in front of a car driven by Bud Henderson. He was unable to avoid them and they were killed instantly. When a second car driven by Frankie Bailey swerved to avoid the wreck, it struck the fence, killing on spectator and injuring three.

The Fourth of July,1939,proved to be a much more pleasant day at Langhorne. This was the date of the tracks first stock car race. Bill Schoop took the checkered flag,but the next day Mark Light was declared the winner. Light was a spectator who,when he saw the cars warming up, became so enthused that he leaped into a friend's Buick and drove it onto the track. He joined the field in thirty-eighth position, but quickly charged to first for the win.

With it's circular design and surface of dirt and oil, Langhorne was one of the most exciting and treacherous tracks in the country for many decades.

Back in the South, the series' at Daytona and Atlanta continued on into 1940. On September 3 of that year Buck Mathis of Saint Augustine, Florida won the Daytona beach race, where Bob Flock came in ninth. Apparently all the luck was with Bob's brother. On the very same day, Fonty Flock won a 100 mile race at Lakewood,with a time of one hour, thirty-three minutes, and forty-five seconds. He did so despite having turned his car over at one point in the event. The top four that day was rounded out by Gene Comstock of Chesapeake, Ohio, Bud Seithe of Dayton,Ohio, and Red Singleton of Atlanta.

The second World War, of course, brought stock car racing to a screeching halt. At the conclusion of the conflict,however, it didn't take long for the engines to be re-fired. On Labor Day, 1945 , a race was scheduled for Lakewood, that along with competition would bring controversy.

The editors of Atlanta area newspapers and local ministers had begun a campaign against stock car racing. Their complaints stemmed from the fact that many of the participants, including Roy Hall and Bob Flock, had extensive police records. They were also concerned that these young men who were capable of piloting a race car were apparently unfit for military duty. Lastly, they wondered if, in an age of rationing, it was proper to expend rubber and gasoline on a sport that was known to be populated by bootleggers.

In the end it was the voice of the people that was the loudest. A crowd of 30,000 was on hand for the event. Pressure from the police on promoter Mike Benton caused a delay to the start and the throngs of people became unruly. Eventually, the race started with a full complement of drivers. The winner, in what could have been a scripted moment, was Roy Hall.

The second place finisher in this race was Bill France, and October, 1945 would find him promoting a race at the Fairgrounds in Charlotte, North Carolina. This was one of France's first promoting forays away from his base in Daytona. The winner of this race was Bob Flock.

On April 14,1946, just eight months after the end of World War II, racing returned to the beach course in Daytona. In a 160 mile stock car competition, Red Byron drove his Ford to victory lane with a speed of 80.2 miles per hour. Byron was a native of Anniston,Alabama who walked with an pronounced limp. Prior to the war he was known to the Flocks and other drivers as the premiere mechanic in Atlanta. After the war he climbed behind the wheel and became their competition.

Throughout 1946 France promoted races throughout North and South Carolina and Virginia. Though he did so under the aegis of the National Championship Stock Car Circuit, these events were often staged by risking France's personal assets. In spite of competition from other promoters and an inability to always attract the top tier racers, these races were largely successful, with drivers such as Glen Dunaway, Buddy Shuman, and Marshall Teague taking the checkered flag. During the warm months of 1947 he would extend his reach to new markets such as Birmingham,Alabama, and even staged races in New Jersey and Rhode Island. France had now established himself as the premier stock car racing promoter in the Southeast, if not the nation, and he was poised to realize a dream which he had been nurturing since before the war.

The final manifestation of Bill France's dream was brought to fruition on December 14,1947, when a meeting took place in the Ebony Bar atop the Streamline Hotel in Daytona. France was part owner of the bar. Those present included Red Byron, Red Vogt, Buddy Shuman, Marshall Teague, and Frank Mundy. When the group endeavored to name itself, Red Vogt suggested "National Association For Stock Car Automobile Racing", but this was voted down. However,once modified to "National Association of Stock Car Auto Racing", the vote passed and NASCAR was born. France suggested that E.G. "Cannonball" Baker, famous as a racer and stunt driver,be the group's first commissioner. The men then elected Bill Tuthill as secretary, Eddie Bland as vice-president, and Marshall Teague as treasurer. Bill France, of course, was elected president.

The first race sanctioned by the group was run on February 15,1948. This was a beach race in which the top three finishers were, in order, Red Byron, Marshall Teague, and Bob Flock. On February 21 NASCAR became a corporation in the state of Florida. The first race sanctioned after this was in Jacksonville, Florida, on February 24. The top three in this event were Fonty Flock, Bob Flock, and Red Byron. In all of 1948 NASCAR sanctioned fifty-two races, nine of which were promoted by Bill France. Though no series champion was named, the unofficial title went to Fonty Flock by virtue of his fifteen victories.

In all of 1949, NASCAR would sanction eighty-seven races. Events were held at twenty-five different speedways, and

$181,289 in prizes were awarded. Eight of these races saw the introduction of a new division, the Grand National division. The only vehicles that were qualified were unmodified, late-model, American made cars. The removal of headlights and bumpers were the only alterations to the cars' showroom condition that were allowed.

The first of these races was held at the Charlotte Speedway in North Carolina, and Lee Petty was determined to participate. Petty was born on March 14,1914, near Randleman, North Carolina. Petty spent the first two years after World War II indulging his passion for automobiles. By fine tuning engines along with his brother, Julie, Petty became a dominant force in the impromptu drag races which were held on local highways. Unlike the regions bootleggers,who were driven by necessity, Petty learned to beef up engines and handle cars simply for pleasure.

In 1948 Lee and Julie decided to join the professional ranks. They bought a 1937 Plymouth in which they promptly installed a Chrysler straight-eight engine. That first year they racked up several victories and their winnings totaled $900. This represented a net loss, however, and Petty's racing career seemed on the verge of failure. Fortunately, the first Grand National race in Charlotte presented him with an irresistible temptation. To qualify, he convinced a friend to loan him an unblemished 1948 Buick. In addition to Julie, Petty's "crew" consisted of his sons, Richard and Maurice. The entire family made the trip from Randleman to Charlotte in the Buick that Lee would run in the race. The number he used that day, and later would make famous, was 42. Supposedly, it was picked at random off a junk license plate in the Petty's yard.

Petty easily qualified for a field that included some of the premier drivers of the day. As cars fell out of the race, Petty moved steadily towards the front. Suddenly, a sway bar broke, and the Buick rolled over four times. Petty himself was unhurt, the worst damage being perhaps to his ego. He would have to invest in a 1949 Plymouth in order to finish out the season.

The first to cross the finish line that day was Glenn Dunaway. NASCAR, however, took it's mission to reform the sport very seriously. When brackets which were designed to increase handling in the corners were discovered attached to Dunaway's springs, he was promptly disqualified. This resulted in an official top five of Jim Roper, Fonty Flock, Red Byron, Sam Rice, and Tim Flock. Dunaway filed suit against NASCAR, but the case was dismissed. This was one of the first of many failed lawsuits against NASCAR.

The fourth place finisher that day, Sam Rice, was also a partner in another of the tracks that hosted a Grand National event in 1949. The Martinsville Speedway, in Martinsville,Virginia, is the only track that hosted Grand National races in 1949 and still appears on NASCAR's top division schedule today. At .52 miles it is also one of the shortest tracks on the circuit.

Rice had once won at Daytona in a 1942 Mercury, and this served as inspiration for his friend, H. Clay Earles. Earles imagination was also stirred by radio broadcast of the Indianapolis 500. In fact,the track would host a single AAA race for open wheeled cars, but Earles eventually decided that the closer proximity of the NASCAR drivers would help keep costs down. However,the final motivator for Earles, Rice,and their friend Henry Lawrence,was a trip to a dirt track race in Salisbury, North Carolina. This was in 1947,and the modest crowd they saw that day convinced them that stock car racing had a bright future. They decided to become business partners in a new track, which they would finance with a $10,000 investment from each man. It is widely suspected that this money had been acquired through the sale of illicit alcohol. A minimum of this was spent on grading the facility since Rice also happened to own the earth moving equipment that was necessary.

The inaugural race was on September 7,1947.Although 5000 seats were planned, only 750 were in place for opening day. This did not deter 6,013 people from paying $2 a head for admission. In addition to this, so many people from nearby farms wandered over to the track, that the actual attendance was closer to 12,000. Part of the hype was generated by none other than Bill France. He had toured the track while it was under construction and had been impressed. He agreed with Earles and his partners to help advertise the race and bring in some big names from Georgia. In exchange France took twenty-five percent of the gate.

One advertising claim was that the track would be dust free. To achieve this, thousands of gallons of excess oil and water were poured on the track. However, it only took the racers a few laps to expose the futility of this exercise. A huge red cloud of dust, so large that it was visible from miles away, was churned into the air. The spectators were literally covered in dirt. To add insult, many of them had come directly from church in their Sunday best.

In 1948 the full 5000 seats were installed, and in 1949 the track hosted it's first Grand National event.

Outside of NASCAR, a venerable facility was becoming a hotbed of post-war stock car racing in 1948. The "Milwaukee Mile" was a one mile dirt track at the Wisconsin State Fairgrounds in West Allis, Wisconsin. Built originally for horses, the track is first known to have existed in 1876.

In 1891, the farm on which it was located was bought by the state of Wisconsin and became the State Fair. The first auto race was in 1903 and concrete retaining walls were added in the '20's. In 1929 promotional chores were assumed by Tom Marchese. Throughout the '30's, Marchese brought some of the biggest names in racing to Milwaukee. During this same period the Green Bay Packers played several games on the track's infield. The first stock car race was on August 22,1948. In this 100 mile event, the winner was Paul Bjork of Minneapolis. With a speed of 65.217 mph, Bjork was originally thought to have come in second. However, a scoring error discovered after the checkered flag gave Bjork the victory. His winnings were a very stout $1,878.

Another track utilized in 1949 which also became a mainstay on the Grand National circuit was the North Wilkeboro Speedway, in North Wilkesboro, North Carolina. At .62 miles it too was one of the shortest tracks in Grand National racing. It is thought to be the first stock car track built with any significant banking in the turns. Due to natural topography it was also out of level, with competitors racing slightly downhill into turn one and slightly uphill into turn three.

It was the brainchild of Enoch Staley who was known to be involved in the illicit liquor business. His brother Gwyn and some of his friends were always racing their bootlegger cars anyway, so Staley decided he might as well see if he could make a buck off of it. He approached Bill France who assured him that if he built a track NASCAR would schedule a race there. France made the trip from Daytona to show the fledgling facility how to stage a race. Expected attendance for the first event was three thousand, but ten thousand showed up and North Wilkesboro was a staple of the NASCAR schedule for decades to come.

The other tracks that held Grand National races in 1949 were in Hillsboro, North Carolina., Langhorne, Pennsylvania, Pittsburgh, Pennsylvania, Hamburg, New York, and Daytona.

Stock car racing also continued in 1949 at Milwaukee, with the same scoring problems as the previous year. First place in a 150 mile race on July 10 was awarded to Myron Fohr, though fans were convinced that Paul Russo or Ed Roston was the real victor. Russo would gain redemption on August 25. Fohr had led 89 of the scheduled 100 laps in this second race, when tire trouble disabled his Lincoln and the second place Oldsmobile of Ray Richards. This cleared the way for Russo, who claimed the checkered flag in his Cadillac with a speed of 67.750 mph.

The Men Behind the Machines-Part 1

Louis Jerome "Red" Vogt was born on September 22,1904 in Washington,D.C. As a young man he moved to Atlanta and opened a garage, and more importantly, met Raymond Parks. Preparing cars for Parks' drivers Red Byron and Roy Hall was Vogt's introduction to stock car racing. In 1941 Vogt's machines dominated the stock car racing world, winning over half of the races they entered and claiming the checkered flag throughout the Eastern third of the nation. Vogt built cars for Parks that won four consecutive races on the beach at Daytona and with Byron driving his cars he won the first NASCAR championship in 1949. He would later work as a crew chief for Carl Kiekhaefer. Drivers who won with his cars and engines include Bob and Fonty Flock, Jack Smith,Roy Hall, Lloyd Seay, Curtis Turner, and "Fireball" Roberts.

30

THOSE FABULOUS FIFTIES

Over the summer of 1950 the Grand National division made new forays into the North. The first of these was at the Canfield Motor Speedway in Canfield,Ohio. Fittingly, the winner was a Northerner. Bill Rexford, a native of Conewango Valley, New York, drove his Oldsmobile to victory on the half mile dirt oval. The next race, on June 18, was at the Vernon Fairgrounds in Vernon, New York. The winner here, in a Mercury, was Bill Blair. The diminutive Blair was born in High Point, North Carolina.

The date for the inaugural "Southern 500" was September 4, 1950. The venue, the Darlington Raceway, a giant paved oval, was unlike anything stock car racing had seen before.
The track was the brainchild of South Carolina native Harold Brasington. He had derived his inspiration from trips he had made to Indianapolis in 1933 and to the old board track in Charlotte. Together with his partner, Barney A. Wallace, he raised about $60,000 in capital. The land for the track was a

seventy acre cotton field, which was donated by Sherman Ramsey in exchange for shares in the newly formed raceway corporation. Ground was broken for the facility on December 13, 1949. Without so much as a blueprint, a tractor was sent into the field to grade out the track. The result was an oval of 1 and 1/4 miles, a distance decided on because it was exactly half the length of Indianapolis. The turns at each end were modeled after those of the area dirt tracks, and were originally banked at about sixteen degrees. Once the entire track was paved, and about 9,500 grandstand seats were added, Darlington Raceway was ready to be christened.

Even more ambitious than the track itself was the event which Brasington and Wallace planned to hold. A 500 mile stock car race had never been attempted before and many doubted if such an idea was viable.

The enormity of the event was evidenced by the qualifying system. A ten mile race was run on the each of the fifteen days leading up to the "Southern 500". The top five finishers in these heats were qualified for the main event. When it was all over, the field consisted of 75 drivers representing sixteen states. While seventeen brands of automobiles were present, Oldsmobile 88's, which numbered twenty-nine, dominated. By virtue of his victory in the first qualifying race, Curtis Turner sat on the pole, while Californian Johnny Mantz brought up the rear. The fastest speed, 82. 35 miles per hour, had been recorded by Wally Campbell of New Jersey. Brasington and Wallace had originally contracted with the Central States Racing Association, a midget car sanctioning body, to sponsor the race. However, when it became clear that the C.S.R.A. was out of it's league, NASCAR assumed promotional responsibilities.

On race day 26,000 fans showed up, and another 10,000 had to be turned away. The crowd was witness to a ribbon cutting ceremony performed by the wife of Governor Strom Thurmond. The green flag dropped at 11 a.m. and the checkered flag would not fall until 6 and 1/2 hours later. The consensus before the race was that the stock engines would not last for 500 miles. Lee Petty had even taken the precaution of bringing an extra engine. The most fallible equipment, however, turned out to be tires. In 1950, everyday street tires were the racing standard, but they were no match for for the combination of high speeds and asphalt. While the bigger, heavier cars could generate higher speeds, they were also susceptible to constant blow-outs.

This worked to the advantage of Johhny Mantz. Starting dead last in a light weight Plymouth, he maintained a leisurely 75 mile per hour pace. This enabled him to conserve tires and gas, thus requiring fewer pit stops. When he did pit, his crew utilized something that previously was unknown in stock car racing: pneumatic lug wrenches. By the time the rest of the field realized the method behind Mantz's madness, it was impossible to catch up to him. When his car, bearing the number 98 JR., crossed the finish line, he was fifteen miles ahead of the second place finisher, "Fireball" Roberts. Mantz's average speed had been 76.26 miles per hour, while fifty-six of the seventy-five starters finished the race.

Apart from being NASCAR's greatest year to date, 1950 also

brought the organization a new challenge as the AAA sponsored it's most ambitious schedule of stock car races to date. Two of these were, of course, at the "Milwaukee Mile".These races were on April 5 and August 24. The first contest was for 150 miles and was won by Myron Fohr in a Lincoln. In the second event, which lasted 100 miles, Norm Nelson finished first in an Oldsmobile. From this point forward, Milwaukee would be the centerpiece of stock car competition on the AAA, and later the USAC, circuit.

On September 4, the same day as the "Southern 500",a 100 mile AAA race had been run at Du Quoin,Illinois. The victor here, driving an Oldsmobile, was J. Frank. The AAA also sponsored a 200 mile race at Lakewood on September 10.Billy Carden won this race in a Mercury.

Three firsts were recorded on June 16,1951, at the Columbia Speedway in South Carolina. It was the first stock car race held under the lights and was the first time a Studebaker found it's way to victory lane. The driver, scoring his first Grand National win, was Frank Mundy.

Also in 1951, a new make of automobile began appearing on the Grand National circuit. The Hudson Hornet was made in Detroit and featured a large displacement, in line, six cylinder engine. Marshall Teague, a driver and mechanic based in Daytona,had convinced the company to provide him with cars,parts, and support, in what was an early example of a factory based team. Hudson would receive tremendous bang for their buck. In the first half of the Fifties, Hudsons were as dominant in NASCAR's top tier as souped up Fords were in the modified ranks.

On July 1,1951 NASCAR made it's first venture outside the United States. This was the date of a 100 mile race at Stamford Park in Niagara Falls, Ontario. The winner, in a Hudson, was Buddy Shuman.

On July 15 ,1951, one of the big races on the AAA circuit was run at Milwaukee. The field included Hudsons, Oldsmobiles, Packards, Nashes, Studebakers, Lincolns, Cadillacs, and one Ford. All of these were put to shame, however, by the Chrysler of Tony Bettenhausen. Bettenhausen managed to lap every driver, some of them two or three times, except Rodger Ward, who was driving an Oldsmobile. Then with less than thirty miles to go, Bettenhausen began experiencing clutch problems. This caused his car to lurch from his pit before it was fully fueled. When he stopped again just six miles from the checkered flag, Ward was able to take the lead. He then held off the charging Bettenhausen and collected $3,225.

In the Spring of 1951 NASCAR made it's initial forays into the West. A Grand National race was held on April 8 at Carrell Speedway, a half mile dirt track in Gardena, California. Another was run on April 22 on the one mile dirt track at the State Fairgrounds in Phoenix, Arizona. Both of these races saw Marshal Teague drive to victory lane in his #6 Hudson.

1952 would see competition not just between drivers, but also between sanctioning bodies. The AAA, which had sanctioned three stock car races in 1951, raised the number to seventeen in 1952. In addition, two prominent NASCAR drivers, Marshall Teague and Frank Mundy, were persuaded to defect to AAA. Mundy had developed ill feelings towards Bill France, while Teague wanted a shot at the Indy 500 and what he presumed would be larger purses

Throughout 1952, the Hudson Hornet dominated competitions on the AAA circuit much as it did in Grand National racing. With NASCAR firmly entrenched in the South, most AAA races were in Mid-Western locations such as Toledo, Ohio, Williams Grove, Pennsylvania, Milwaukee, Wisconsin, Dayton, Ohio, Terre Haute, Indiana, and Springfield,Illinois. There were also forays out to the West coast in such towns as Pomona,California,Gardena,California, and Klamath Falls, Oregon. Marshall Teague picked up victories at Toledo,Williams Grove, Milwaukee, and Dayton on his way to the AAA championship.

Back on the Grand National circuit, Herb Thomas made a late season charge for the title. Thomas won four of the last six events, including Martinsville, North Wilkesboro, and the season's final race at West Palm Beach, Florida. However, Thomas' efforts would not be enough as the youngest Flock, Tim , emerged on top when all the dust from the '52 NASCAR season had settled. Under the tutelage of older brothers Bob and Fonty, Tim was apparently a quick study. Flock , who started every race except one, finished with 8 wins, 6858.5

points, and $22,890 in winnings.

On the strength of the performances by Tim Flock and Herb Thomas, Hudson easily captured the NASCAR manufacturers title, which was awarded for the first time in 1952.

No West coast facilities appeared on the 1953 Grand National schedule, but NASCAR did take it's elite series to some new locations over the summer months. Races were held on June 7 in Shreveport, Louisiana, on July 22 in Rapid City , South Dakota, on July 26 in North Platte, Nebraska, and on August 2 in Davenport, Iowa. The winners, in order, were Lee Petty, Herb Thomas,Dick Rathman, and Herb Thomas again. These were the first and only Grand National races ever held in these four states.

Herb Thomas became the first two time Grand National champion in 1953, doing so in a completely dominant fashion. He finished with 12 wins, 8,460 points, and $28,910 in winnings. The rest of the NASCAR top ten were Lee Petty, Dick Rathman, Buck Baker, Fonty Flock, Tim Flock, Jim Paschal, Joe Eubanks, Jimmy Lewallen, and Curtis Turner.

A native of Barbecue Township, North Carolina, Herbert Watson Thomas was born on April 6,1923. He attended Ben Haven High School in Olivia, North Carolina, after which he took over his father's sawmill. He supplied the military with lumber during World War II, and didn't begin racing until after the war.

In 1953 the Midwest Association of Car Racing was formed. It was later renamed and is much more well known as the Automobile Racing Club of America, or ARCA. The inaugural season saw races in Ohio,Michigan,and Pennsylvania. A winner at one of these events was Lee Petty's brother, Julie.

In a group which included the Flock brothers and Glen Dunaway, to stand out as a hell raiser and troublemaker was no small feat. The one man who did so, always with a dash of style, was Curtis Turner. Though Turner never won a championship, his exploits on and off the track, along with his occasional feuds with Bill France, cemented a reputation that survives to this day.

Turner was born on April 12,1924, in Floyd County, Virginia. He stood six feet, two inches, and weighed 220 pounds, but is remembered as a lover and not a fighter. His father was both a manufacturer and purveyor of illicit liquor. Turner is alleged to have made his first liquor run at the age of ten. At fourteen he dropped out of school to work as a water boy in his father's sawmill. By eighteen he had made enough money hauling liquor to buy three sawmills of his own. He would remain involved in the timber industry for the rest of his life.

When World War II erupted Turner enlisted in the Navy.

Incorrigible as always, he helped himself to tires at the Naval Air Station in Norfolk, Virginia, and transported them back to his friends in the mountains.

After the war he began to test his driving skills against those of other Southerners. His first race was in Mount Airy, North Carolina, in which he finished eighteenth in a field of eighteen. His first victory, however, came in his very next race. It was during this period that Turner earned the nickname "Pops". This was supposedly derived from the sound of two stock cars banging together, a sound to which Turner was no stranger. One of his trademarks was that he likewise referred to everyone he encountered as "Pops".

Francis Eduardo Menendez was born June 8,1919, in Atlanta, Georgia, and spent his formative years at an orphanage in Macon. At the age of seventeen he began driving cars and motorcycles for Lucky Teeter's Hell Drivers, a traveling daredevil and stunt show. His most outlandish stunt was crashing a motorcycle through a wall of flaming burlap. By this time his friends in Atlanta had distilled his name into Frank Mundy. He spent most of 1938 and '39 driving for Jimmy Lynch's Death Dodgers at the World's Fair in New York. Though he had met Bill France in Daytona in the late thirties, it was not until after World War Two that his stock car career began in earnest. He competed against the best of the early drivers, such as the Flock brothers and Curtis Turner, and was part of the group which helped France form NASCAR at the Seabreeze Hotel. He also raced in the first strictly stock race sanctioned by NASCAR in 1949.

1953 would be another big year for Hudson as Hornet drivers would capture both the AAA and NASCAR titles for the second year in a row.

The AAA circuit visited most of the same tracks as in '52, and added stops in Phoenix, Arizona, Heidelberg, Pennsylvania., Syracuse, New York, and Winchester, Salem, and Fort Wayne, all in Indiana. The championship would go not to Teague, but the other NASCAR expatriate, Frank Mundy. Mundy posted two wins at Gardena, California, as well as one each at Toledo, Heidelberg, and Milwaukee. In his number 7 Hornet, with a Confederate battle flag emblazoned on the side, he must have been regarded with more than just curiosity at many of these tracks.

The fourth edition of the "Southern 500" was run on September 7,1953. This race saw a dramatic increase in speeds, as Buck Baker drove his Oldsmobile to the checkered flag at an average speed of 92.881 mph. Six days later, an Oldsmobile was back in victory lane at Central City Speedway in Macon, Georgia. The winning driver at Macon that day was Alfred "Speedy" Thompson. Thompson was born in Monroe, North Carolina on April 3,1926.His father and brother were both racers, but would each die young from a heart attack, the same fate that awaited "Speedy". However, in '53 "Speedy" was still in his prime, and he scored his second Grand National victory on October 11 at North Wilkesboro.

One week later, at Martinsville, another first time winner was added to the record book. James Roy Paschal was born on December 5,1926, in High Point, North Carolina. He started racing in 1947, but competed only occasionally as he preferred the steady paycheck he earned as a furniture re-finisher. 1953 was his first full Grand National season and his first win came in a Dodge.

On February 21, 1954, at Daytona's beach race, it was Lee Petty and Chrysler in victory lane. Petty's switch from Dodge came almost by accident. During the off season he had borrowed a friend's new Chrysler for a test drive. He had been so impressed with the machine that he insisted on buying it on the spot. Petty was actually second to Tim Flock that day, but Flock was disqualified because of an illegal carburetor. Flock felt that this was a flagrant attempt by NASCAR to showcase the new Chryslers. He was so incensed that he virtually dropped off the circuit for the rest of the year. In any event, the name Petty would forevermore be associated with Daytona.

A Hudson which still fared well was that driven by Marshall Teague on the AAA circuit. One of his victories in '54 came at Milwaukee, where the the one mile dirt track had been paved. His   total of five victories would be enough for the AAA championship

Also in 1954, NASCAR would expand it's reach all the

way from Florida's coast to that of California. Under the aegis of Bob Barkhimer ten Western tracks were added to the NASCAR schedule. On March 28 Dick Rathman took his Hudson Hornet to the winner's circle at a 125 mile race at Oakland. Another example of these new facilities was the one mile Bay Meadows dirt track in San Mateo. Here, on August 22, first place in a 250 mile event went to Herschel McGriff and his Oldsmobile.

After almost a decade of service,the Martinsville speedway was paved in 1955.

The first race in 1955 was at West Palm Beach on February 6. A victory here by Herb Thomas marked the last time a Hudson Hornet would appear in victory lane at a Grand National event. The Hudson Motor Car Company was on the verge of a merger with Nash-Kelvinator that would result in the formation of AMC, and the Hornet would disappear from stock car racing as quickly as it had come to dominate it. However, Hudson would have one last hoorah. In the final year of AAA involvement in stock car racing , the title was won by Frank Mundy.

The Hornet Mundy drove to that last championship was owned by a gentleman named Carl Kiekhaefer, who was the son of the founder of the Mercury outboard motor company. On the NASCAR circuit in 1955 ,Kiekhaefer would field several of the new 331 cubic inch Chryslers. Though car owners such as Raymond Parks had been around since before the war, Kiekhaefer's '55 campaign was the genesis of the modern race team. He maintained an entire fleet of vehicles, dressed his pit crews in matching uniforms, and tried, though not always successfully, to maintain discipline among his drivers. Depending on who you ask, Kiekhaefer was either an innovative genius or an obsessive tyrant. He went so far as to have his engineers collect dirt samples from the various tracks to aid in the setup of his cars. This led to the development of the paper based oil filters that are still the standard today. Kiekhaefer's influence on stock car racing cannot be overstated.

The star of Kiekhaefer's operation was Tim Flock. After his self imposed exile, Flock found himself a new job through a chance encounter on the beach in Daytona with an associate of Kiekhafer's. For the running of the beach race in '55 Flock put his new boss' Chrysler in the pole position, next to the Buick of "Fireball" Roberts. This situation became reversed after 160 miles, as Roberts took the checkered flag. However, in a bizarre repeat of the previous year, Roberts was found to have illegal push rods. Flock was the beneficiary this time, and was awarded the win the following day. His speed was 92.05 mph.

Though Hudson would win the title,Chrysler was also beginning to make its mark on the AAA circuit in 1955. However, at a July 16 race at Milwaukee a little luck was needed. Norm Nelson had assumed the lead in the 150 mile event with less than 25 miles to go. As he tried to hold off the Chevrolet of Marshall Teague, Nelson was watching through a hole in the floorboard as his right front tire was gradually shredding. An instant after he crossed the finish line the tire exploded with an enormous boom, and Nelson was sent crashing into the wall. He was unhurt, though, and was able to collect his $3,864 in winnings.

Due to a spate of on track fatalities, 1955 would be the last year that AAA sponsored any type of racing. The resulting void was filled in part by the 1956 formation of the United States Auto Club, or USAC.

In addition to sanctioning the '56 Indy 500, USAC also sanctioned stock car races, mostly at the same Mid-Western tracks that had hosted AAA events. In June, USAC also held a 500 mile stock car trial at Indianapolis, thus beating the NASCAR stocks there by thirty-eight years. At this event the tandem of Chuck Stevenson and Johnny Mantz , driving a Ford, posted a speed of 107.12 mph.

Over the next three decades USAC would sanction events from coast to coast on every type of track. These races also provided an introduction to the world of stock cars for such big names as Fred Lorenzen, Paul Goldsmith, A.J. Foyt, Parnelli Jones, and Mario Andretti. NASCAR regulars such as Ralph Moody, Curtis Turner, Darrell Waltrip, and even Richard Petty also participated.

Marvin Panch was born in Menominee,Wisconsin on May 28,1926. After dropping out of high school he and his family moved to Oakland, California where he had a brief boxing career and got his start in racing. He won California late-model titles in '50 and '51, then served two years in the Army. Once discharged, he yearned to try his luck on the Grand National circuit , so he made the move East to Charlotte.

Paul Goldsmith was born October 2, 1925, in Parkersburg, West Virginia, but his family soon moved to Michigan because of the availability of jobs on the automobile assembly line. Before coming south, he served in the merchant marine , raced modifieds at some Midwestern tracks, and was a three time champion of the American Motorcycle Association. In one of his first NASCAR races, Goldsmith gained instant respect from the Southern drivers when he finished second to Curtis Turner after rolling his car one complete turn. One of his first NASCAR wins was on September 23,1956 at Langhorne, Pennsylvania, where he drove a #3 Chevrolet to victory. He holds the distinction of being the only person to win both a motorcycle and stock car race on the beach at Daytona. When several manufacturers drop out of NASCAR in the late fifties, Goldsmith eventually landed on the USAC circuit where he won the championship in 1962 and '63.

The 1956 Grand National championship was fraught with controversy. With the season nearing it's end, the chances for Buck Baker to catch Herb Thomas in the points battle were becoming fewer and fewer. It was perhaps a personal grudge against Thomas that led Baker's car owner, Carl Kiekhaefer, to rent the Cleveland County Fairgrounds in North Carolina. He then pressured Bill France to insert an extra date into the schedule. During this race Kiekhaefer's other driver, Speedy Thompson, seemed to intentionally wreck Herb Thomas. Thomas sustained injuries that were so severe he missed the final three races of the season. Baker easily, though some would say illegitimately, won the title.

The first race of calender '57 was the beach race at Daytona which was held on February 17. This was the first Grand National victory for Pontiac.

Buck Baker was also in the winner's circle on August 4, 1957 as NASCAR made another foray onto a road course. Watkins Glen is a resort town near New York's Lake Seneca. As a tourist attraction, races were run through the streets of the town in the years immediately after World War II. This tradition had to be abandoned after a series of fatal accidents. An interim track was used in the early fifties, but was replaced by the 2.3 mile, eleven turn course that remains today. The track was designed by Bill Milliken with the help of Cornell University's computer department. While it is a fixture on the NASCAR circuit today, Grand National racing did not return to Watkins Glen for nearly a decade after Baker's '57 victory.

On the same day as the Watkins Glen race, a Grand National event was held at Kitsap County Airport in Bremerton, Washington. The winner, in a #11 Ford, was Parnelli Jones. He was born Rufus Parnell Jones on August 12,1933 in Texarcana, Arkansas, but his family soon migrated to California. While he competed mainly on the USAC and SCCA circuits, he also claimed several NASCAR victories of which the Bremerton race was his first.

On July 12,1958, the Grand National race at Asheville, North Carolina was won by Jim Paschal. It could be argued that this race was not as significant as one that took place in Columbia, South Carolina. While Lee Petty and his son, Maurice, went to Asheville, Lee's other son, Richard, along with his cousin, Dale Inman, went to compete in a convertible race in Columbia. Richard had petitioned Lee to let him race a few years earlier, but had been told to wait until he was twenty-one. After Richard's twenty-first birthday, Lee consented, and provided the younger Petty with a '57 Oldsmobile. Richard tuned up the convertible then painted the now famous number 43 on the side. His rationale was that 43 was next in sequence after Lee's number 42. Though his qualifying effort was average, Richard coaxed the Olds around Columbia's dirt surface to a sixth place finish.

One of the most colorful and tragic racing figures of the late Fifties and early Sixties was "Little" Joe Weatherly. Joseph Herbert Weatherly was born in Oak Grove,Virginia., on May 29, 1922. When he was nine his father died, rather ominously, in an automobile accident. Afterward the family moved to Norfolk where Joe delivered newspapers. He was drafted into the Army in 1942 and served in North Africa, where his two front teeth were shot out by a sniper. After the war he began racing motorcycles and was a three time champion of the

American Motorcycle Association. He began racing stock cars in 1950 when came to regard bikes as too dangerous. Throughout his NASCAR career he was known as an incessant prankster and permanent sidekick to Curtis Turner. Weatherly's favorite gag was to present a box to his victims which he claimed contained a mongoose. In actuality it was squirrel's tail attached to a spring, which would seem to leap out when the box was opened

The Grand National race which was run on May 7 ,1955 at Hickory, North Carolina was won by a man who in racing lore is nothing short of a legend. Bill France had long desired to disassociate NASCAR from the illicit liquor industry. However, the relationship between the two would be forever cemented by Junior Johnson. Born Robert Glen Johnson, Jr., in 1932 in Wilkes County, North Carolina, he had come from a long line of moonshiners. He began hauling the family's wares at the age of fourteen. In 1953, Junior, along with his father,brother, and two hired hands, was indicted and convicted of several felony charges. However, Junior won an appeal and never had to serve the 18 month sentence. Aside from driving ability, Johnson also honed some of his mechanical skills during these years. One of his early innovations was to scour the junkyards of the Piedmont in search of Chrysler ambulances so he could mount their oversized engines in his lightweight Ford liquor cars. His initial Grand National victory at Hickory came less than two years after his 1953 conviction. Proving that this was no fluke Johnson went on to win four more races in 1955.

Johnson would not be on hand for most of the 1956 season, however, due to a previous engagement. Though Junior never was caught while transporting liquor, he did have the extreme misfortune to be at his father's still when it was raided one day in '56. The senior Johnson had served time on several previous occasions, but in this instance it was Junior himself who happened to be there when the revenuers came to call. He was sentenced to two years and a $5000 fine, the time to be served at the federal prison in Chilicothe, Ohio. He was released for good behavior after ten months and three days, but was compelled to serve another thirty days when he was unable to pay the $5000.

By 1958 he would be free and back behind the wheel of a race car. He won six races in '58 in a Holman-Moody prepared Ford, the first win coming in truly sensational style. At the May race at North Wilkesboro, Johnson slid over the earthen bank in one of the turns and actually left the race track. Undeterred, Johnson stayed in the gas and coaxed his car back over the bank, onto the track, and to the checkered flag.

By 1959, due largely to the efforts of Bill France, stock car racing had experienced not only a   reformation, but also a transformation. Still greater changes were imminent, however, as France   was about to unveil what was unquestionably the crowning achievement of his career: the Daytona International Speedway. The giant track would be a harbinger of things to come, as two more super-speedways would open the following year, effectively sounding the death knell for major dirt track racing.

As early as 1949 residents of Daytona Beach were growing wary of the noise, traffic, and crowds associated with a major racing event. Though France endeavored to appease all parties, it was obvious that a new facility was necessary if racing was to survive in Daytona. City and county officials had formed the Racing and Recreation Facilities Authority on August 16, 1954, in order to explore possibilities for a new track. This body signed a contract with a corporation headed by France, called the Daytona Motor Speedway Corporation, on June 6, 1955. This contract called for a facility to be built with $2,500,000 in bond money and operated by DMSC.

However, a sluggish economy prevented a sufficient amount of bond money from being raised. By 1957, the RRFA was reorganized as the Speedway District Commission. This group signed a new contract with DMSC, allowing the corporation to lease the land that had been selected and to begin construction. The tract that had been chosen was 4.5 miles from the beach and adjacent to Daytona's airport. Ground was broken on November 25,1957.

This left France scrambling for financing. $300,000 was raised by selling stock in the corporation, while France himself borrowed another $600,000. An arrangement was made for the Pure Oil company to have the grading done in the center of the track, which was necessary to provide the banking in the turns. This left a forty-four acre pit in the earth which today is Lake Lloyd. One initial roadblock was that no one could be found who had paved such a steep bank before. A trio of contractors, Pat Bolton, Muse Womack, and Walter Manley, agreed to tackle the problem and were able to get the job done.

The result was a giant asphalt tri-oval, a design based partially on the Fulford-Miami Speedway,a board track that had operated in the Twenties. The track was 2.5 miles long, the exact length of the Indianapolis Motor Speedway. What made Daytona different from Indy was the extreme 31 degree banking, the likes of which had not been seen since the halcyon days of the board tracks.

To the old time dirt track drivers, to whom Darlington had been awe inspiring, Daytona must have been absolutely intimidating. The track was christened with two forty lap qualifying sprints on February 20, the first of which was won by Bob Welborn in a Chevrolet. Welborn was a native of Greensboro,North Carolina., who normally competed in the convertible division , and had been named it's champion in '56,'57,and '58. The second qualifier was won by "Shorty" Rollins. This put Welborn and Rollins in the front row for the first 500 on February 22, with a field of fifty-seven more cars behind them. A distinct feature of Daytona became immediately apparent to the drivers. A car traveling in the wake of the car in front of it had a distinct advantage as the vehicles entered the corners, while the car leading the pack was impeded. A clever driver could learn to turn the physics of Daytona to his advantage- a technique that would soon be dubbed "drafting". The two drivers who correctly deciphered the track on that inaugural day were Lee Petty and Johnny Beauchamp. Beauchamp was an Iowan who had won the IMCA championship previously, and had been lured to Daytona by the record $67,760 in prizes. Petty, in an

Oldsmobile, and Beauchamp, in a Ford, were neck and neck as the race drew to a close. Pacing them was the car of Joe Weatherly, who was one lap behind. The three crossed the finish line in a dead heat and the checkered flag was shown to Johnny Beauchamp. He appeared in all the papers, clutching the first place trophy in victory lane.

However, Daytona's reputation for controversial finishes had long before been established. After three days, during which Bill France conducted an intense perusal of still photo and motion picture evidence, Lee Petty was declared the winner of the first Daytona 500. It would not be the last time, however, that he and Beauchamp would cross paths on Daytona's high banks.

The Men Behind the Machines-Part 2

A native of Tennessee, Henry "Smokey" Yunick grew up dirt poor during the depression. His father died young and Yunick had to go to work at a very early age in a garage to help support his family. As a teenager he would compete in motorcycle races on a bike whose thick exhaust earned him the nickname "Smokey". He claimed that he bought a fake birth certificate in order to join the military and didn't know what his real name was.

After serving as a fighter pilot during World War Two he eventually found his way to Daytona where he opened his own garage. It seemed only natural that he would become involved in racing. From the early fifties through the mid Seventies cars that he owned were entered in 76 races in NASCAR's elite division. As a mechanic he worked on ten cars that competed in the Indianapolis 500 and won NASCAR's championship in 1954 with Herb Thomas. He was also at constant odds with NASCAR officials. Yunick once brought a dominant car to Daytona that outwardly appeared perfectly legal. It was eventually discovered to be a 7/8's replica. This led to the use of templates to inspect the cars. On another occasion NASCAR disassemble one of his entries so completely that the gas tank was removed. Yunick showed his disgust and cemented his legend by driving the car away.

Ray Fox was born in Salem,New Hampshire in 1916. As a child he attended races at the local board track and recognized some of the drivers as the same men who routinely set land speed records at Daytona.

He honed his mechanical skills during World War II by working on Jeep engines. After the conflict he made the trek south to Daytona and found work at Fish Carburetor. During this period he would race himself, but found it too expensive an undertaking, so he began preparing cars for others to race. One client was Herb Thomas, one of the few drivers who could compete with Tim Flock in 1955. Team owner Carl Kiekhaefer noticed this and hired Fox away for his own team. Fox also had his own garage by this time and would routinely tune up Junior Johnson's liquor cars.

In 1957 Kiekhaefer suddenly left racing and Ray Fox found himself unemployed. Out of necessity he started his own race team and over the next decade and a half would win races with Buck and Buddy Baker, Junior Johnson, and David Pearson.

ALL IN THE FAMILY

One family in particular not only paved the way for the many brother combinations that would populate racing over the years, they were also instrumental in creating the stereotype of stock car racers as hell raising good ol' boys. The Flock brothers were the real deal. Bob,Fonty,and Tim were three of eight children from Fort Payne, Alabama. Robert Newman was born April 16,1918, Truman Fontell was born March 21,1921 and Julius Timothy was born May 11,1924.Their father was a bicycle racer and stunt man who is said to have owned the first car in Fort Payne. Tragically,cancer claimed his life in 1929,leaving his eight children to survive on the nine dollars per week that their mother earned in a hosiery mill.

In the days before government entitlements, family was the only possible source of help. Help came in the form of an uncle with the improbable name of Peachtree Williams. Williams invited the oldest Flock,Carl,to Atlanta to help with his bootlegging operation. Carl accepted,and proved so adept that he was soon in business for himself. This enabled him to bring his siblings to Atlanta one by one. Once there,Carl saw to it that they were provided for and adequately schooled.

Before long Bob and Fonty were old enough to help Carl with the family business. They began hauling moonshine after school. A typical run was to Dahlonega, in the North Georgia mountains, and back. A successful run paid forty dollars and, on a good day, two runs could be made. Tim was too young to drive but frequently got to go along for the ride. Occasionally he was employed to fling gallon jugs of liquor out the window and into the windshields of pursuing police cars.

Bob Flock is the subject of a tale which, apocryphal or not, just has to be one of the all time great stock car legends. The City of Atlanta had passed an ordinance which prohibited anyone who had been caught hauling liquor anywhere in Georgia from competing in races within the city limits. The law certainly applied to Atlanta's famed Lakewood Speedway. For the Labor Day, 1947 race, it was no secret that Bob Flock had qualified for the race, but he had managed to sneak into the track and was ensconced in his car on the starting grid with a bandanna to hide his face. An officer spotted him, however, and approached his driver side window. At this point Flock put his car into gear and cruised slowly over to the backstretch and came to a stop. Without delay two motorcycle cops were dispatched around either end of the track to corner him. Unfazed, Bob bolted from a dead stop, down the backstretch, and through the fence in turn three. A race through the streets of Atlanta ensued, which Flock naturally won. He did, however, turn himself in a few days later and was fined a total of $136.00.

Beginning in mid-August,1952, the Flock brothers laid claim to a distinction which they will probably always have. They remain to this day the only trio of brothers to win three consecutive Grand National events. The streak started on August 15, when Tim won a rain shortened race at Rochester, New York. Next into victory lane was Bob, who finished first at Weaverville, North Carolina. The third race in the streak was the crowning achievement of Fonty Flock's career. On September 1, Fonty won the "Southern 500" in an Oldsmobile owned by Frank and Sara Christian. Irrepressible as always, Fonty had driven to his greatest triumph in a pair of Bermuda shorts

Along with his brother Bobby, Donnie Allison was part of what is arguably the most successful brother team in stock car history. He was born Donald Joseph Allison on September 7, 1939 in Miami,Florida. A natural competitor just like his older brother, Donnie was a statewide diving champion in high school.

In the mid-Sixties he followed Bobby into the Grand National circuit, and also like Bobby he was soon logging victories. His first win was at Rockingham in 1968. The biggest year of his career was 1970. In this campaign he drove Banjo Matthews' Ford to wins at Bristol,Charlotte, and Daytona. He would continue to run a limited schedule and score sporadic victories for the rest of the Seventies. His last win was at Atlanta in November,1978, and an accident at Charlotte in 1981 essentially ended his career.

Bobby and Donnie were followed by Bobby's sons, Davey and Clifford. Both of them died tragically and it is unclear if a future generation of Allison's will ever compete in a Cup race.

Sterling Marlin was another second generation driver. His father, Coo Coo Marlin, was a regular on the Winston Cup circuit throughout the Seventies. Sterling was born on June 30,1957, in Columbia, Tennessee. After a high school football career he turned to racing. In his first Winston Cup year, 1976, he earned $565 for a single start, then ran his first full season in 1983. He met with limited success through a series of owners over the next decade.

He eventually teamed with Morgan-McClure Racing and won back to back Daytona 500s in 1994 and '95. Before his career ended he would also notch victories at Talladega and Darlington.

While other families may have more victories , when it comes to shear numbers its hard to beat the Wallace clan.

The most famous and most successful among them is of course Rusty. A native of Fenton, Missouri, Rusty cut his teeth on the tracks of the Midwest. It was there that he earned Rookie of the Year honors on the USAC circuit in 1979 and was ASA champion in 1983. During this same period he would make occasional forays into NASCAR, including a 1980 debut at Atlanta where he piloted Roger Penske's Chevrolet to a very impressive second place finish behind Dale Earnhardt.

He would team with owner Cliff Stewart in 1984 for his

first full time Winston Cup campaign, racing his way to Rookie of the Year once again. A switch to owner Raymond Beadle brought his sole NASCAR championship in 1989. In 1991 he would re-team with Penske and rack up impressive win totals for the rest of his career.

Mike Wallace was born March 10,1959 and followed in Rusty's footsteps. He debuted in the Busch series in 1990 and has been a regular competitor there ever since. He made his Cup debut in 1991 at Phoenix. Since Rusty and younger brother Kenny also appeared in this race, it marked the first time that three brothers had competed in NASCAR's top level since the Flock brothers almost four decades before. Mike has remained winless at the Cup level but has scored several victories in the Busch\Nationwide series and in NASCAR's truck series.

Kenny Wallace was born August 23,1963. He started his career as a crew member for Rusty then climbed behind the wheel in the ASA,where he was Rookie of the Year in 1986. He graduated to the Busch series in 1988 and won Rookie of the Year in 1989. While he has competed intermittently at the Cup level, he has made over 400 starts in the Busch\Nationwide series, where he has scored several wins. He still competes on occasion but is also well known as a racing commentator on television.

Rusty retired after the 2005 season and today ,like Kenny ,is a racing analyst on TV. He also owns a team that competes in the Nationwide series. His son Steven drives for this team full time while Mike's daughter Chrissy makes occasional starts for the same team. Mike and Chrissy both raced in a Truck series race in 2009, marking the first time that a father-daughter tandem had competed in a NASCAR race.

Dale Jarrett holds a distinction that can be claimed by no one else except Richard Petty. They are the only two champions of NASCAR's top division whose father's were also champions. Dale didn't seem interested in following in Ned's footsteps in his younger days. Instead of racing he preferred football and golf. At the former he had no shot at turning pro, at the latter, maybe.

The racing bug did eventually bite him, however, and he made his Winston Cup debut at Martinsville in 1984. A succession of second tier rides followed for the rest of the Eighties until he was given the chance to platoon with Cale Yarborough as the former champion contemplated retirement. Finally, in 1990 Neil Bonnett's misfortune would prove to be Jarrett's good luck. When Bonnett was seriously injured in a crash at Darlington Jarrett was tapped to replace him in the famed Wood brothers' # 21.

In 1991 Jarrett would score his first victory after an epic battle with Davey Allison. The two sons of champions battled door to door for lap after lap before Jarrett finally prevailed by less than a foot. The next year he made what seemed like a questionable decision to join a brand new team. This team, however, was owned by someone who knew a little about winning: former Washington Redskins coach Joe Gibbs. Jarrett would place the unproven ride in victory lane at the 1993 Daytona 500. Not pretending for a moment to hide his emotions in the broadcast booth was his proud father,Ned.

Jarrett's next career move was again determine by the bad luck of someone else. Barely a year after replacing the late Davey Allison, Ernie Irvan was very nearly killed in an accident at Michigan. At the outset of the 1995 season Jarrett climbed into a car that seemed positively cursed. He seemed to be leading a charmed existence, however, as he guided the # 28 to victory at Pocono that summer. When Irvan returned in 1996, team owner Robert Yates formed a new team which was built around Jarrett. It was in this new #88 that he would attain his greatest success. In the first year Jarrett won his second Daytona 500, the Coca-Cola 600 at Charlotte, the Brickyard 400, and a 400 mile race at Michigan.

Phil Parsons, Benny's younger brother, was born June 21,1957, in Detroit, Michigan. His first and only Winston Cup win came on May 1 in the "Winston 500" at Talladega.

The Labontes are a pair of racing brothers from Corpus Christi, Texas. Terry is the older and in terms of championships the more successful. He found early success on the dirt tracks of East Texas, but when he moved to Charlotte to accept a job on the team of fellow Texan Billy Hagan, it was as a crew member, not a driver. In 1978 Hagan had a falling out with his driver which provided Labonte with sporadic opportunities to prove himself. He made the most of his chance and by 1979 he had earned the ride full time. Though his first full campaign was impressive he lost Rookie of the Year honors to Dale Earnhardt. In 1984 Labonte would provide Hagan with his only championship. He then moved on to a succession of owners and near oblivion. In 1993 he paired with owner Rick Hendrick and by 1996 this pairing would produce Labonte's second title, improbably coming twelve years after his first.

Younger brother Bobby started racing go karts in Texas, but moved to North Carolina when Terry ascended to the Cup ranks. Here he worked in Terry's race shop, competed locally on the Modified circuit, and made occasional starts in the Busch series. By the early 90's he was fielding his own full time Busch team and won the title in 1991. He graduated to Cup competition with Bill Davis Racing in 1993 and in 1995 he moved to Joe Gibbs Racing. Success came immediately as Bobby scored his first Cup win in the "600" at Charlotte. He would remain a consistent winner for the rest of the decade, culminating in a Cup championship in 2000. To date, Bobby is the only driver to win both a Busch\Nationwide title and a Cup title. Also, Terry and Bobby are the only brother tandem to win Cup championships.

The Bodines are a trio, Geoff, Brett, and Todd, of brothers who hail from upstate New York. Their father and grandfather built a small race track in Chemung, New York, and it was here that Geoff got his racing start. As a teenager he once allegedly disguised himself as a girl to run a Powderpuff race. He soon graduated to Modifieds and was track champion at several facilities in the Northeast. From there he graduated to the Grand National division of NASCAR and finally to Winston Cup. He is by far the most successful of the brothers with a total of 18 Winston Cup wins the biggest of which was the 1986 Daytona 500.

Brett and Todd would follow Geoff into NASCAR racing, but things were not always familial. Geoff and Brett once infamously wrecked each other while running first and second in the Brickyard 400.

Today Geoff owns a company that designs and builds bobsleds. His sleds have won several medals, including a gold, for the U.S. in Olympic competition. Todd has found a home as a consistent contender and frequent winner in NASCAR's truck series.

The Burton brothers are a racing duo that hail from South Boston, Virginia. Ward was born October 25, 1961 and Jeff was born June 29 ,1967 . Jeff made it to the Busch series first in 1988 and won Rookie of the Year in 1989. Ward debuted in the Busch series in 1990. Jeff debuted in the Cup series in 1993 and won Rookie of the Year in 1994 driving for the Stavola Brothers team. He would join Rousch racing in 1996 which is where he has enjoyed his greatest success. Notable wins have come at Darlington, Charlotte, and the inaugural race at Texas Motor Speedway. In 2000 , after the deaths of Adam Petty and Kenny Irwin, Jr., a race was run at New Hampshire in which plates were required. Jeff Burton won the race by leading every lap. Currently he drives for Richard Childress Racing where he is consistently competitive and an occasional winner. Jeff is a talented driver who knows how to take care of quality equipment. However, to date a Cup title has eluded him.

Ward graduated to Cup racing in 1994. Though he has fewer wins than his younger brother, some of them have been prestigious. Ward can claim victories in both the Southern 500 and the Daytona 500. Today Ward is retired from racing and as a well known outdoors man he is spokesman and sponsor for several conservation groups.

Combining on track heroics and off track histrionics, the Busch brothers have plenty of attitude but back it up with ability. Kurt was born August 4, 1978, and as the son of a racer was in a go kart at an early age. He then moved on to Legend cars and full size cars in NASCAR sanctioned events at local tracks in the Southwest. He performed well enough to earn what was essentially an audition with Rousch Racing. Busch made an impression and graduated to NASCAR's truck series. Here he won Rookie of the Year honors and was waging his first full Cup campaign by 2001.

By 2002 Busch had found his way to the winners circle, notching his first victory at Bristol. He has proved to be an absolute master at this track, at one point winning four events in a row there. In 2004, when NASCAR debuted it's Chase format, Busch became the first to win a championship under the new system. He continued to be almost unstoppable at tracks such as Bristol and New Hampshire during this campaign. In 2006 Busch replace another short track master when he took over Rusty Wallace's famous #2 for Penske

South. Though a second title has eluded him Busch remains a consistent contender.

Kyle Busch was born May 2, 1985, and in a series that some say lacks personalities, has become one of the most electrifying and polarizing figures since Dale Earnhardt. His early career mirrored Kurt's to a degree, so much so that after go karts and legends cars he graduated to driving on the Truck series for Jack Rousch. However, after NASCAR imposed a minimum age requirement in 2002, the sixteen year old Busch was forced to make forays into ASA and ARCA.

When Kyle returned to NASCAR in 2003 it would be as a driver in the Busch series for Rick Hendrick. In 2004 he was Rookie of the Year at this level. By 2005 he had graduated to Nextel Cup and found victory lane twice on his way to winning Rookie of the Year. He scored several more wins for Hendrick before moving to Joe Gibbs racing in 2008. There he became the first driver to score a victory for Toyota when he won at Atlanta. Kyle is an iron man of sorts, frequently competing in all three of NASCAR's top divisions and routinely scoring multiple wins in the same weekend. In a feat that would cause Tim Flock and Richard Petty some envy, Busch is the only driver to win in two of the top three divisions on the same day. With an abundance of talent, nerve, and youth, it seems impossible that Kyle will not someday join his brother Kurt on the list of NASCAR champions.

THE SWINGING SIXTIES

A first was realized February 28,1960 when Richard Petty, who had won his first convertible race the previous year at Columbia, got his first Grand National win. It came at the Charlotte Fairgrounds, where Petty and his Plymouth reached victory lane with an average speed of 53.40 mph.

In 1960 NASCAR would contribute to the spirit of the new decade by debuting two new super speedways and it's first new champion in four years.

The first of these tracks was the Charlotte Motor Speedway in Charlotte,North Carolina. One of the principal figures in it's construction was O. Bruton Smith. Smith, a native of Oakboro,North Carolina., began his business career as a car dealer. After promoting his first race at the Midland Dustbowl in Midland, North Carolina, he continued to promote races at tracks throughout the region.

Smith had the unlikeliest of partners: none other than Curtis Turner. While Lee Petty would channel most of his winnings back into his racing enterprise, Turner considered himself a businessman of a different sort. He had engaged in a series of wildly speculative deals, most notably in the timber industry, and, at least on paper, had been quite successful.

However, neither Smith nor Turner had the two million dollars which they estimated would be required to build their super speedway. They were undeterred, though, and construction began, utilizing the type of creative financing at which Turner was an expert. A significant portion of the money was raised by selling shares in the speedway corporation to 1400 stockholders. Expenses rose when the tract of land they had selected proved to be rife with veins of granite, which had to be blasted away. A solution was always found for these dilemmas, however. Turner even went so far as to buy a small town bank through which he could make loans to himself. On another occasion, a contractor who was irate over not being paid, used tractors to block the path of the paving machines. A remedy for this problem was found when Smith and Turner produced a shotgun and a pistol, thereby persuading the contractor to back down.

The end result of all this mayhem was a 1.5 mile track with turns banked at 24 degrees. Today the Charlotte Motor Speedway is one of the premiere facilities in all of racing.

The situation in Atlanta was somewhat different. At 1.522 miles and with the same 24 degree banking, the Atlanta International Raceway would originally have a paper clip shape but would be reconfigured decades later to include a dog leg in the front stretch. It would also be rechristened the Atlanta Motor Speedway. While the price tag was also the same two million dollars, the financial backing was somewhat more stable. Construction was also easier because the track was situated in a natural bowl in the ground.

Another similarity was that both tracks spelled doom for their predecessors. While Grand National racing would stay on at the Charlotte Fairgrounds for two more years, Lee Petty's win in June of '59 marked the last Grand National race at Atlanta's famed Lakewood Speedway.

The Charlotte Motor Speedway was inaugurated on June 19, 1960 with an unprecedented 600 mile race. The race was won by Joe Lee Johnson, driving a Chevrolet, with a speed of 107.73 mph. It was Johnson's second victory and would also be his last.

Although the event drew a healthy crowd, it also produced more problems for the plagued facility. The track had been built so hastily that the asphalt had not had time to cure, causing it to blister when the behemoth stock cars began racing around it. This sent the track into deeper financial trouble.

Though super speedways were quickly overtaking stock car racing, the 1960 Grand National title went to a driver without a single victory on the big tracks. Rex White would win his only championship with 21,164 points. Behind him , Richard Petty had catapulted to second place. The rest of the drivers in the top ten were Bobby Johns, Buck Baker, Ned Jarrett, Lee Petty, Junior Johnson, Emanuel Zervakis, Jim Paschal, and Banjo Matthews.

In 1961 NASCAR would have more exposure and controversy than it had seen in some time. One new wrinkle was the emergence of Pontiac in the "factory wars" that Detroit was beginning to wage on the nation's race tracks. Having finished no better than fourth in the manufacturers points previously, Pontiac would leap into second in '61. This was accomplished by winning thirty of fifty-two races with drivers such as "Fireball" Roberts, Joe Weatherly, Marvin Panch, Cotton Owens, and Junior Johnson.

Pontiac was dominant from the outset of the season, with Roberts and Weatherly winning the twin qualifying races at Daytona. In the race which Weatherly won, Lee Petty and Johnny Beauchamp re-staged their battle from two years before, this time with near fatal consequences. Three laps from the end of the race, Petty's and Beauchamp's fenders became locked and both cars actually flew out of the speedway. Amazingly, both drivers survived . At the 500 itself, run on February 26, the winner was Marvin Panch, also in a Pontiac. There were no cautions in the race, pushing Panch's average speed up to 149.60 mph. Pontiac would rack up two more super speedway victories at Marchbanks Speedway on March 12 and Atlanta on March 26. At Marchbanks, the last NASCAR event held there, the winner was "Fireball" Roberts. At the 500 mile race at Atlanta, Bob Burdick won with a speed of 124.17 mph.

A soon-to-be-famous newcomer got his first win at Martinsville on April 9,1961. Scheduled for 500 miles, the event was halted due to rain and the declared winner, in a Ford, was Fred Lorenzen. He had been born December 30,1934, in Elmhurst, Illinois. His first race was a demolition derby at Soldiers Field in Chicago. He then moved to NASCAR Modifieds and later to USAC late models, where he was series champion in 1958 and '59. He had dabbled in Grand National racing before but it was not until 1960 that he made the move full time. His second foray was in a car he built with two buddies in the restaurant business. It was financed by Lorenzen's father and with a loan that unknowingly came from the Mafia. He returned to Illinois with nothing to show for his efforts but $7,000 in Mob debt.

His fortunes would swing , however, before the year ended. Lorenzen climbed into the Holman-Moody Ford in 1961,after receiving a famous Christmas Eve phone call from Ralph Moody, and this combination would produce twenty-six wins before he retired in 1967.

Two 100 mile races were run at Charlotte on May 21, 1961.In the first, Richard Petty picked up his second win of the season, his first having come at Atlantic Rural Fairgrounds in Richmond,Virginia. The second feature was won by Joe Weatherly. In what now appears as another eerie coincidence for Weatherly, this was the same day that NASCAR staged it's first competition at Riverside International Raceway. Riverside was a 3.3 mile road course which was about fifty miles east of Los Angeles and had opened in 1957. At this first Grand National race the winner was Lloyd Dane in a Chevrolet. It was the last of Dane's four victories, all of which came at West coast tracks.

One week later, at the second "World 600", Pontiac picked up another win with a virtual unknown at the wheel. David Gene Pearson was born December 22,1934. In his first race in 1952 he was awarded a whopping $13. He labored on the Modified circuit for eight years before stepping up to Grand National in 1960, driving his own Chevrolet. At the "World 600", Ray Fox had brought a Pontiac to Charlotte with no one to drive it, and was persuaded to give Pearson a chance. He was rewarded with a victory as Pearson took the checkered flag with a speed of 111.63 mph.

While some of the old time drivers never managed to adapt to the super speedways, Pearson was apparently born to them. On July 4, at Daytona's "Firecracker 250", Pearson picked up his second career win, again in a Pontiac. In a caution free race his speed was 154.29 mph. This was also an especially significant race for NASCAR. As evidence of stock car racing's growing legitimacy, this became the first NASCAR race to appear on nationwide television when ABC broadcast it as part of it's "Wide World of Sports" program.

By 1964 he had moved to Cotton Owens' team and scored eight wins that year. Due to the dust up between NASCAR and Chrysler, Pearson spent most of 1965 on the USAC circuit, but he returned to win the Grand National Championship in 1966. He would finish out the decade driving for Holman-Moody, scoring twenty seven wins in '68 and '69 and titles in both years.

On July 30, 1961, the inaugural race was run on a track that is still a mainstay of the circuit today. Bristol International Raceway is technically in Tennessee, but is within a stone's throw of the Virginia state line. At .533 miles it is the second shortest track on the NASCAR circuit. It has been reconfigured over the years, and today features 36 degree banking which is the steepest of any track in America. At that first 250 mile race, the winner was Jack Smith, driving a Pontiac, with a speed of 68.37 mph.

One last bit of fallout from 1961 came in November, when Charlotte Motor Speedway filed for bankruptcy. The court ordered that the reorganization be overseen by a committee of stockholders. One of the first actions of this committee was to dismiss Bruton Smith and Curtis Turner. Turner would have no further involvement with the speedway, but Smith would return as it's owner years later.

Ned Miller Jarrett was born in Newton,North Carolina, in 1932. His first driving experience was taking the family car to church at the age of nine. Like many other drivers from the region, he found his first employment in the lumber business. His first race was in 1952 after he became part owner of a car in a poker game. His parents objected so vehemently to his new career path that he once ran a race under an assumed name. He ran the 1955 Southern 500, where he finished last , and so for the next two seasons decided to hone his skills in the Sportsman division.

Though known for his calm demeanor, Jarrett financed his return to Grand National racing in 1959 in a manner that can only be described as outlandish. He wrote a $2,000 dollar check for what he felt was a winning car late on Friday after the banks had closed. Over the weekend he was able to claim checkered flags at Myrtle Beach, South Carolina and Charlotte, North Carolina. With the winnings from his new set of wheels he was able to cover the check by Monday morning.

Jarrett won the Grand national championship in 1961 and 1965. His second title run was highlighted by a victory in the Southern 500. He won this race by a jaw dropping 14 laps over Buck Baker. This is a record that still stands today and most likely always will. He also had run much of the season with a plastic brace enclosing his lower back after a severe accident on a dirt track in Greenville,South Carolina. Jarrett retired in 1966 with fifty Grand national victories.

The glamor and high speeds associated with the super speedways were now becoming common place. However, the 1962 championship would be won the old-fashioned way: on short tracks in small Southern towns. Most of Joe Weatherly's nine wins would come on tracks of a mile or less in towns such as Asheville, North Carolina, Augusta, Georgia, Savannah, Georgia, and Chattanooga, Tennessee. In the first of his two titles Weatherly would garner 30,836 points. The top ten was completed by Richard Petty, Ned Jarrett, Jack Smith, Rex White, Jim Paschal, Fred Lorenzen, "Fireball" Roberts, Marvin Panch, and David Pearson.

The 1963 NASCAR season would see the beginning of a

tradition that would last almost twenty years. Today the first race after the winter layoff is in February at Daytona. However, from '63 to '81 this was preceded by a January race at the Riverside International Raceway in California. The first of these races was won by a stranger to NASCAR. Dan Gurney would collect five Grand National victories in his career, all of them at Riverside. He had been born Daniel Sexton Gurney on April 13, 1931, in Port Jefferson, New York. After his family moved to Riverside,California., he took up drag racing, even once running at the Bonneville Salt Flats. He then took up sports car racing before joining the Army and serving in Korea. He returned to racing after his discharge,and when Riverside was built in 1957 he was one of it's first competitors. He then moved up to Formula 1 racing and ran at the Indianapolis 500. When the NASCAR drivers came to call in 1963 , Gurney was lying in wait for them , a veteran of the type of road racing with which they were all but ignorant. Although Paul Goldsmith sat on the pole, Gurney clearly had the fastest car in practice. On race day the only Grand National regular who seemed able to grasp the course was "Fireball" Roberts. However, Gurney passed Roberts just beyond the halfway point, then cruised to victory in his Ford. Gurney would dominate the Grand National races at Riverside until his retirement.

In February of 1963 Daytona became the scene of a great deal of drama. The twin qualifying races were won by Junior Johnson and Johnny Rutherford, both of whom drove Chevrolets. Rutherford was a Texan and a transplant from the

USAC circuit. In addition to the 500, the speedway was also scheduled to host several other races, including a sports car race dubbed the "Daytona   Continental". One of the entrants in this race was Marvin Panch, driving a Ford-Maserati hybrid. During a practice session, Panch lost control of the car at an estimated 180 mph and it immediately burst into flames, with Panch trapped inside. Several bystanders raced to the crash site, lifting the burning car so that Panch could escape. Among Panch's rescuers was Tiny Lund.

Lund was born DeWayne Louis Lund in Harlan,Iowa. He began racing motorcycles and midget cars, but due to his enormous size was practically forced to move to stock cars. He had existed on the periphery of the Grand National circuit for years, even subbing for Junior Johnson while Johnson was in prison. He had come to Daytona that year without a car, hoping to garner interest from any team. Then fate intervened in the form of Marvin Panch. Panch had been slated to drive the Wood brothers' Ford in the 500, but was unable after his crash. As a reward , Panch petitioned to have Lund replace him, and the Woods agreed.

On race day an enormous storm blew in and the start was delayed for two hours. When the green flag finally fell the early going was dominated by Chevrolets. After a series of Chevy engine failures, however, the lead was assumed by a string of five Fords, led by Fred Lorenzen. In the final laps Lorenzen and Ned Jarrett had to pit for fuel. This gave the lead to Lund, who had conserved fuel by drafting behind the others. He coasted into victory lane, where the car had to be re- fueled in order to drive it to the garage. The $25,850 prize was split three ways because Lund and the Wood brothers had previously agreed to each give ten percent to Marvin Panch. The top five finishers, all driving Fords, were Lund, Lorenzen, Jarrett, Nelson Stacy, and Dan Gurney.

The second half of the 1963 season would see "Fireball" Roberts win his second "Southern 500" with a speed of 129.784 mph. Fred Lorenzen would win the fall events at Bristol and Martinsville, while Marvin Panch, back from his injuries, would win the fall race at North Wilkesboro. The season would end with a 400 mile race back at Riverside, which was won by Darel Dieringer in a Mercury. Dieringer was a native of Indianapolis who got his start racing convertibles and USAC stock cars. He worked for a brief period at NASCAR events as an employee of Firestone.

Richard Petty would finish the '63 season with thirteen victories, more than any other driver. Unfortunately, he would finish second in points to Joe Weatherly for the second year in a row. Weatherly would finish with only three wins but 33,398 points, more than 2000 more than Petty. Both were probably envious of the third place finisher, Fred Lorenzen. Lorenzen was the top money winner with $113,750, making him the first NASCAR driver to have more than six figures in winnings.

In 1964, Bill France invited ARCA founder John Marcum, a long time associate and one time employee, to bring his series to Daytona. An ARCA sanctioned race has been part of speed weeks ever since.

1964 was NASCAR's most ambitious campaign to date, and perhaps ever. In all there would be a mind boggling sixty-two Grand National races. Before the schedule was half complete, however, stock car racing would be dealt two severe blows.

The first was the death of Joe Weatherly on January 19. Well liked by the public and his competitors, the reigning champion would lose his life in a crash at Riverside. The stock car community had barely recovered when tragedy struck again in May. In the early stages of the "600" at Charlotte, "Fireball" Roberts was severely burned in a terrifying crash. He would linger until July, but then the man who was probably NASCAR's most popular driver was gone as well.

When the 1964 season was finally over, Richard Petty emerged with his first championship. It came exactly ten years after his father,Lee, had won his first title. Although Ned Jarrett and his Ford recorded six more victories than Petty and his hemi-powered Plymouth, Petty's 40,252 points put him more than 5,000 point ahead of the second place Jarrett. In a season that many were probably glad to see end, the rest of the top ten were David Pearson, Billy Wade, Jimmy Pardue, Curtis Crider, Jim Paschal, Larry Thomas, Buck Baker, and Marvin Panch.

Having survived the tumult of 1964, NASCAR would be tested once again in 1965. A controversy would erupt in the off season, even before the first green flag. Ford had complained about Chrysler's hemi for all of '64. To negate the Chrysler advantage, Ford wanted permission to use it's own racing engine which featured a single over-head cam shaft. An elaborate ruse was carried out in which Bill France was taken on a tour of a bogus assembly line. The intent was to convince France that the over-head cam engine was a standard production item, but he was not fooled. He did, however, make a huge concession to Ford by banning all hemi engines for the 1965 season.

This backed the Dodge and Plymouth drivers into a corner. Some, like Junior Johnson, merely switched to Ford while others defected to the USAC circuit. Richard Petty, however, found a third alternative. With his team invested heavily in Plymouth machinery, Petty decided to build a hemi-powered behemoth, then embarked on a drag racing career. This meant NASCAR was faced with the loss of it's reigning champion and most popular driver.

Mario Gabriele Andretti was born on February 28,1940, in Montona,Italy, along with his twin brother, Aldo. The brothers had raced Fiats as teenagers in Italy, and after moving to Nazareth, Pennsylvania., in 1955, naturally found themselves competing in the local Modified races. Aldo dropped out of racing after a serious accident, but Mario continued , racing midget cars and Modifieds. His initial foray into USAC racing came in 1964. In 1965 he won the USAC title in his first full season, then repeated in 1966

With the hemi banned from NASCAR, Fords driven by

Marvin Panch, Fred Lorenzen, and Junior Johnson dominated the first half of the 1965 Grand National season. Then, on July 31, at a half-mile paved track in Nashville,Tennessee, a race was won by a manufacturer other than Ford for the first time since February 12. The winning driver was none other than Richard Petty. Several factors contributed to the return of NASCAR's prodigal son. One was that Petty sensed a growing resentment among the regular NHRA drivers due to all the attention he attracted. This was punctuated by a tragedy that occurred in Dallas,Georgia. Finally, Bill France had softened his position on the hemis, essentially allowing them on short tracks only. On the same day as Petty's victory, while attending a USAC race in Atlanta, France announced that Petty would not be the only wayward driver returning to NASCAR. Almost four years after it was imposed, France had decided to lift the suspension of Curtis Turner. As was the case with Petty,concern over low attendance probably affected France's decision. Turner's return to the Grand National circuit came on August 8 at Asheville-Weaverville Speedway in Weaverville, North Carolina. The race was won by Petty , while Turner was forced out with mechanical difficulties.

A final noteworthy event remained for the 1965 season: the swan song of Curtis Turner. The old-timer's first Grand National win since 1959 came on a brand new track. The North Carolina Motor Speedway was built near Rockingham,North Carolina. It was the brain child of Harold Brasington, of Darlington fame. The paved track is 1.017 miles long and features banking as steep as 25 degrees. At the inaugural event on October 31 all of the top finishers were Fords. The fastest of all was Turner, who got his final victory with a speed of 101.942 mph while driving a #41 Ford that had been prepared by the Wood brothers. He did so with a broken rib he had sustained during a previous race at Charlotte. Though he won hundreds of modified races on the dirt tracks of the South, his total victories on the Grand National circuit numbered seventeen.

At the outset of the 1966 season peace had been restored to NASCAR, but it would be short lived. The ban on Chrysler's hemi had been lifted, but Ford was still insisting that it be allowed to compete with it's single over-head cam engine. Ford demanded that the situation be resolved by April, but it would remain up in the air as the season got underway. However, there was one positive development off the track. Goodyear had produced a new safety tire which was now required on all Grand National cars. It consisted of a hard inner lining inside the tire that would support the weight of the car in the event of a blowout.

The first driver to win the Daytona 500 twice was Richard Petty in 1966.Run on February 27, the race was halted with two laps to go due to rain. By that point Petty had outdistanced the field and was declared the winner.

The spring race at Atlanta in 1966 was won by someone unknown to NASCAR fans, Jim Hurtibise. Hurtubise was a native of Tonowanda, New York., and a veteran of the USAC circuit. A crash in 1964 resulted in burns that threatened his life, but he was back behind the wheel by '65. The win at Atlanta was his only Grand National victory.

In May of 1966 Bill France announced his decision concerning Ford's single over-head cam engine. He agreed to let Ford race the engine, but imposed a one pound per square inch penalty. This essentially put the Ford's at a 427 pound disadvantage. Without making as big a show as Chrysler had the previous year, Ford quietly withdrew it's factory support. Some drivers moved to other teams while others would struggle on as independents. Ned Jarrett, the reigning champion, would eventually take this as his cue to retire.

Bobby Allison got his initial Grand National win at a 1/3 mile track in Oxford, Maine on July12,1966.

After all the complaining, Ford still won the manufacturers' championship in 1966, although Dodge and Plymouth had more points when the two were combined. Chrysler also won the drivers' title with the Dodge of David Pearson. Pearson won his first championship with 35,638 points and fifteen wins. He was followed by James Hylton, Richard Petty, Henley Gray, Paul Goldsmith, Wendell Scott, John Sears, J.T. Putney, Neil Castles, and Bobby Allison.

In a career that was essentially one triumph after another, most of Richard Petty's seasons pale when compared to 1967. In early March, fate began to smile on Richard Petty, and he was launched into a streak that will probably never be equaled. On March 5, he won a 300 mile event at Weaverville, North Carolina, and was the most consistent winner on the circuit for the next five months. Along with wins at short tracks across the South and at tracks in New Jersey and New York, he claimed victories at Martinsville, Darlington, Rockingham, and Bristol. The 400 mile event at Darlington was the fifty-fifth of his career, placing him on top of the all time list, one win ahead of his father,Lee. He was on such a roll that in a 200 mile race in Nashville on July 29, he came back from an eight lap deficit to win by five. As the summer entered it's final months, Petty was just beginning to get warm. On August 12, he won a 250 lap race at Winston-Salem,North Carolina, then reeled off three more wins to tie the record for consecutive victories. The fourth win came on September 4, in the "Southern 500". With a speed of 130.423 mph, it was his only first place finish in the famed event. He promptly broke the record the following week with a win at Hickory,North Carolina. A string of five more firsts set the new mark for consecutive victories at ten. The final two had come at Martinsville and North Wilkesboro. There was no doubt the season would end as a complete blow-out for Richard Petty.   He finished the season with 42,472 points, more than 6,000 ahead of the second place finisher. He also collected a staggering $150,196 in winnings. Even today, his marks of twenty-seven wins in a season and ten consecutive wins seem unassailable. The remainder of the top ten were James Hylton, Dick Hutcherson, Bobby Allison, John Sears, Jim Paschal, David Pearson, Neil Castles, Elmo Langley, and Wendell Scott.

While Richard Petty was cementing his name in the NASCAR record book in 1967 , Iggy Katona was doing the same on the ARCA circuit. Katona was born on August 16,1916 in Toledo,Ohio, and served in the Army during World War Two. He competed in the first year of MARC/ARCA racing and won three titles in the Fifties. In the Sixties he would win three times at Daytona as well as collect three more titles, the last coming in '67. That same year he set ARCA records for oldest winning driver and total wins.

One of the few drivers who is as prominent in the NASCAR record books as Richard Petty is David Pearson. In 1968 Pearson would have his greatest season in terms of wins, though he he was not quite as dominant as Petty had been the year before. In March Pearson racked up his first two victories of the year at Bristol and Richmond,Virginia. Pearson had switched late in '67 from the Dodge that he drove for years to a Ford. The car was owned by Holman-Moody and former driver Dick Hutcherson served as crew chief. In May , Pearson scored four consecutive wins, three on short tracks and one in Darlington's "Rebel 400". The points system had been overhauled since the previous year, so David Pearson won his second title with a total of only 3,499. He also had sixteen victories, the most of his career. Second place went to the resurgent Bobby Isaac, while Richard Petty, who also had sixteen wins, came in third. The rest of the top ten were Clyde Lynn, John Sears, Elmo Langley, James Hylton, Jabe Thomas, Wendell Scott, and Roy Tyner. Cale Yarborough, who finished seventeenth , had the most winnings, with $138,064.

The 1969 season was perhaps one of the strangest in the history of NASCAR. The tone was set at the beginning of the season when Chrysler introduced it's new Dodge Daytona. The car was powered by the standard hemi, but was unusual it that the rear deck featured a raised winged spoiler. Chrysler had decided to make the Dodge the focus of it's '69 campaign. This created extreme dissatisfaction with Plymouth's best known proponent, Richard Petty. Petty had requested alterations to the Plymouth for '69, but the factory had declined. The end result was that the entire Petty Enterprises team switched to Ford for the only time in it's existence. In addition to his new role as Ford driver, Petty also found himself in the role of union boss. A new effort to organize the drivers was underway, this time under the moniker of the Professional Drivers Association. As it's first president, the newly formed group elected Richard Petty. Rumors circulated that a boycott was in the works, possibly at the "Southern 500". Some of the PDA's demands were centered around health insurance, pensions, and better facilities in the garages. Their biggest gripe, however, was that the race purses provided them with substantially less pay than other professional athletes.

On June 15,1969 the inaugural race was run at one of four new super speedways. The Michigan International Speedway was a two mile D-shaped oval with an unusually wide surface and eighteen degree banking. It's first Grand National race was a 500 mile event which Cale Yarborough won with a speed of

139.254 mph.

On July 6, 1969 the first Grand National race was run at the brand new Dover Downs International Speedway in Dover,Delaware. The track was a one mile oval with twenty-four degree banking. The 300 mile race was won by Richard Petty.

On August 22, 1969 Richard Petty became the first driver to record 100 wins with a victory at Bowman-Gray Stadium in Winston-Salem,North Carolina. Today he is one of only two drivers to reach this plateau.

Though he had six fewer wins than Bobby Isaac, David Pearson won his third championship in 1969 with 4,170 points. This made him the first three time champion since Lee Petty. He also set a new mark for winnings, with $229,760 in prizes. The top ten was rounded out by Richard Petty, James Hylton, Neil Castles, Elmo Langley, Bobby Isaac, John Sears, Jabe Thomas, Wendell Scott, and Cecil Gordon.

The Men Behind The Machines
Part 3

Bud Moore was born on May 25,1925 in Spartanburg, South Carolina. He served in World War II and landed at Utah beach on D-Day. Before he left Europe he would be awarded five Purple Hearts and two Bronze Stars.

His first big success in racing was as crew chief for Buck Baker, who won the Grand national championship in 1957. Moore would move on to field Pontiacs as a car owner and would win two Grand National titles in the early Sixties with Joe Weatherly as his driver. He is believed to be the first owner to install two way radios to communicate with his driver during a race.

Other notables who would drive for Moore over the years include "Fireball" Roberts, David Pearson, Cale Yarborough, Bobby Isaac, Dale Earnhardt, and Darrell Waltrip. Moore would rack up sixty-three wins as an owner in his Grand National and Winston Cup career.

Everett "Cotton" Owens was born in Union, South Carolina in 1924. A Naval veteran of World War Two, he was an early associate of Bud Moore who made his debut on the the local tracks in the late Forties. By 1950 he had graduated to Grand National racing where he would ultimately score nine victories. Even before his retirement in 1964 he was already fielding cars for other drivers. He was known for several safety innovations, including horizontal bars added to the roll cage to reinforce the driver's door. A veritable who's who of drivers piloted his cars over the years including Ralph Earnhardt, Marvin Panch, "Fireball" Roberts, Junior Johnson, David Pearson, Bobby Allison, Bobby Isaac, Charlie Glotzbach, and Buddy Baker.

BETCHA DIDN'T KNOW

In the late 1940's a group of businessmen and drivers grow disenchanted with with the inconsistent nature of rules, prizes, and promotion. So they band together in a new sanctioning body that will attempt to bring order to the confusion that is the stock car world. Sounds familiar, right? But is it what you think?

The National Stock Car Racing Association was incorporated in Georgia on March 27,1947. It promoted a limited schedule of events in 1948 and crowned Buddy Shuman as it's champion. In 1949 a slew of new promoters, Bruton Smith among them, enabled the NSCRA to promote a more ambitious schedule, though most races were in Georgia, North Carolina, and Tennessee only. Ed Samples won the championship in this second campaign. By 1950 the organization would attract appearances by such big names as

Jack Smith, Gober Sosebee, Bob Flock, Red Byron, Curtis Turner, and Speedy Thompson. Buddy Shuman repeated as champion that year.

However, the NSCRA's days were numbered. Though headquartered in Atlanta, the organization boasted no dominant leader of the stature of Bill France. It's most ambitious member, Bruton Smith, was drafted into the Army in 1950. As a result the various promoters were fighting amongst themselves as much as they were fighting NASCAR. Though a 1951 schedule was initiated, the NSCRA would disintegrate before it reached it's conclusion.

Janet Guthrie and Danica Patrick were hardly the first women to be associated with racing. A native of Barnesville, Georgia, Louise Smith but was born in 1916 and her family moved to Greenville, South Carolina shortly thereafter. She would later marry Noah Smith, who ran a junkyard. While he was away during World War Two Bill France visited the local dirt track and convinced them that they needed a woman in the field to boost attendance. The promoter instantly thought of Louise Smith.

She was loaned a top flight car and finished an impressive third. Bill France was such a believer that he invited her to Daytona the following year. She wrecked before the end of the event but competed on the beach for several more years. She once suffered a horrifying crash during qualifying at Occoneechee Spedway in North Carolina, but still made the start of the race. With above average equipment supplied by her husband, Smith won quite a few Modified events over the years, but her career was winding down just as the Grand National circuit was ascending. Her best finish in NASCAR's top division was sixteenth at Langhorne.

She was joined at the time by Sara Christian, who competed in the first Grand National race in Charlotte. She once ran a beach race in which her husband Frank was entered, making them the only married couple to compete in a NASCAR race. At a race in Pittsburgh she became the only woman to score a top five finish in a Grand National race.

The third well known woman driver of the era was Ethel Mobley. A sister of the Flock brothers, she competed in only two Grand National races. One of these was a beach race, notable because of the presence of her brothers, making it the only Grand National race in which four siblings competed.

Everyone knows that Wendall Scott was the first African-American driver to compete in NASCAR's top division. It turns out that everyone is wrong. In 1956 one of Carl Kiekhaefer's entries at the Daytona beach race was driven by a black racer, Charlie Scott of Forest Park,Georgia. In a field of seventy-six, Scott finished a very respectable nineteenth in his only NASCAR appearance.

Despite Curtis Turner's four wins and Dick Linder's three, neither would win the Grand National championship in 1950. That distinction would be reserved for Bill Rexford. In addition to his one win at Canfield, Ohio he also managed to finish in the top five several times, and was blessed with a little bit of luck. As part of Bill France's campaign for strictly enforced rules, drivers such as Glen Dunaway and the Flock brothers had been disqualified from several races. In addition, many of the Southern drivers did not compete at some of the Northern venues. Rexford, on the other hand, ran almost the entire schedule. This all added up to Bill Rexford's only championship, and afterward he practically vanished from the NASCAR scene. He was followed in the top ten by "Fireball" Roberts, Lee Petty, Lloyd Moore, Curtis Turner, Johnny Mantz, Chuck Mahoney, Dick Linder, Jim Florian, and Bill Blair.

On October 14, 1951, NASCAR staged three Grand National races at three different speedways, a truly ambitious undertaking even for Bill France. The races were at Pine Grove Speedway in Shippenville, Pennsylvania, Oakland Stadium in Oakland, California, and Martinsville. The winners were Tim Flock in an Oldsmobile, Marvin Burke in a Mercury, and Frank Mundy in an Oldsmobile. The following week, Fonty Flock drove the same #7 Oldsmobile as Mundy to a victory at North Wilkesboro.

First place in the April 6 ,1952 race at Martinsville went to the Hudson Hornet driven by Dick Rathman. Rathman was one of two racing brothers from California. His real name was James, but his younger brother Richard, a one time Indianapolis 500 winner, had assumed his identity in order to meet racing age requirements. James in turn adopted his brother's name when he began racing and was known thereafter as Dick.

On June 13, 1954, NASCAR staged it's first ever road race. It was run at Linden Airport in Linden, New Jersey. This was a two mile, five turn course that had long been the scene of many open cockpit races. For what would be the first and for fifty years the only time , a Grand National race featured foreign makes of cars. Racing alongside the Hudsons, Chryslers, and Oldsmobiles were European sports cars, most of them Jaguars. In fact , an XK120 M became the only Jaguar to claim a checkered flag in NASCAR history. It was driven by Al Keller, a mechanic from Bloomfield, New Jersey , and was owned by Paul Whiteman , a popular bandleader of the day. Joe Eubanks and Buck Baker managed second and third place finishes.

A first was recorded on August 3 ,1956 when the Grand National circuit traveled to Oklahoma. Driving a Mercury, Jim Paschal won a 100 mile race at the Oklahoma State Fairgrounds in Oklahoma City. This was the only Grand National race ever held in Oklahoma.

The inaugural Brickyard 400 was not the first time stock cars visited Indianapolis. The United States Auto Club was formed in 1956. In addition to sanctioning the '56 Indy 500, USAC also sanctioned stock car races, mostly at the same Mid-Western tracks that had hosted AAA events. In June, USAC also held a 500 mile stock car trial at Indianapolis, thus beating the NASCAR stocks there by thirty-eight years. At this event the tandem of Chuck Stevenson and Johnny Mantz , driving a Ford, posted a speed of 107.12 mph

July 18, 1958 saw Lee Petty and his Oldsmobile back in victory lane. His win came at the Canadian National Exposition Speedway, a 1/3 mile paved track in Toronto, Canada. This was the second time that NASCAR had ventured outside of the U.S., something that would not happen again for almost forty years.

In August,1958, the AAA stock car circuit made one of its visits to Milwaukee. The 200 mile event was won by Pat Flaherty in a Chevrolet on August 20. Flaherty was a tavern owner from Chicago who had won the Indianapolis 500 in 1956. One month after that triumph he was injured so seriously that the Milwaukee race was his first competition in more than two years. By out-dueling aces such as Dick Rathman and Fred Lorenzen, Flaherty was able to collect $2,882.

At the inaugural Daytona 500 convertibles were allowed to compete alongside the regular stock cars. The open cars were aerodynamically unsound and none of them finished near the top. Though they would never run with the elite machines again, convertibles did compete in their own short lived division.

A third super speedway to appear in 1960 was the Hanford Motor Speedway, alternately known as Marchbanks Speedway, in Hanford,California. This 1.3 mile paved oval was built by

Bonnie Marchbanks, but would close in 1969 and appeared on the NASCAR schedule only in '60 and '61.

At the beginning of August,1961, a controversy which had been brewing for most of the summer finally came to a head. At the center of it was racing's would be tycoon, Curtis Turner. Though only two years old, the Charlotte Motor Speedway was awash in red ink and owed it's creditors about $1,000,000. Turner's unique solution to this problem was to arrange a loan of $850,000 from the Teamsters union. The Teamsters were making inroads into several sports at the time, through an organization called the Federation of Professional Athletes. An agreement was reached whereby the loan would be made if Turner could organize the NASCAR drivers into a local chapter of the Teamsters. Aside from needing the loan, Turner had also become convinced from his experience as a track owner that the drivers were getting short shrift. With the help of Tim Flock he persuaded practically every driver to agree to the union and began to prepare a list of reforms.

However, Curtis Turner and Jimmy Hoffa proved to be no match for Bill France. When France got wind of the union effort he was furious, since he felt that it was NASCAR's role to protect the interests of the drivers. On August 9 France addressed a drivers meeting in Winston-Salem. He threatened to have Daytona plowed under and use his influence to close down the other tracks. He then declared that after that evening's race at Bowman-Gray Stadium, all union members would be banned from NASCAR. This persuaded almost all the drivers to disavow their membership in the union. The two exceptions were Tim Flock and Curtis Turner, both of whom were promptly banned for life from NASCAR. Turner, who had once saved Bill France's life in a Pan American road race, would later be reinstated , but his career was essentially over. Flock simply chose to retire. His last victory had been five years earlier at Road America in Wisconsin.

At the end of July,1955, the Kiekhaefer team accomplished a feat that would give pause to the most well equipped of today's drivers. On July 30 Tim Flock won a 100 mile event in Syracuse, New York. That same day his brother, Fonty Flock, was busy qualifying another Chrysler in San Mateo, California. After the Syracuse race Tim boarded a flight to the West coast. So as not to disrupt the points race, Carl Kiekhafer flew Lee Petty and Buck Baker to California as well. Once in San Mateo, Tim took over his brother's car and led virtually all of the race on his way to yet another victory.

At the start of the '56 season, prior to the now traditional beach race , a NASCAR race was held at the one mile dirt track in Phoenix,Arizona. It was a 150 mile event on January 22, and was won by Buck Baker in a Chrysler. A little more than a month later, on February 26, a NASCAR exhibition was run in Kingman,Arizona. This was the sight of a new five mile test facility that had been built by Ford. The winner of the event, in a Mercury, was Johnny Mantz.

From 1955 to 1969 NASCAR ran races in November and December in which the points awarded were applied to the next year. One such race was run on December 1,1963, in Jacksonville, Florida. The first car to cross the finish line was a Chevrolet driven by Wendell Scott. However, in the post-race ceremonies the promoter gave the first place trophy and $1,000 prize to Buck Baker. The reason for this slight was that Wendell Scott was black. In fact, Scott was the only black racer to ever win on the Grand National circuit and one of the few black men to race stock cars at any level.

Scott was born in Danville,Virginia., on August 29,1921.Through years of hauling liquor the local police managed to catch him only once. This happened on an occasion when he swerved to avoid some pedestrians and lost control of his car, ultimately crashing into a house. When the promoter at the local dirt track asked the cops who might be a candidate to help him attract black patrons, Wendell Scott was their unanimous recommendation. That was in 1947. It took him until 1961 to make it to the Grand National circuit. In the intervening years he and his family, who worked as his crew, suffered innumerable indignities. Frequently the pits were segregated, and at one race in Atlanta Wendell was not allowed on the track until a separate ambulance from a black funeral home was present. Through all this he persisted, and though he only managed a single Grand National victory, he would finish in the top ten several times and in one season earned almost $50,000.

On April 12, 1964 the "Joe Weatherly Memorial 150" was

run at the Orange County Speedway in Hillsboro ,North Carolina, the sight of Weatherly's last win. The winner, in a Dodge, was David Pearson.

On July 10, 1964 the "Fireball Roberts 200" was run at Old Bridge Stadium, a half mile paved track in Old Bridge,New Jersey. The race produced another first time winner in the person of Billy Wade. Wade was a Texan who had first appeared on the Grand National circuit in 1962 and became Rookie of the Year in '63. Driving a Mercury, Wade reeled off four consecutive wins in July of '64. His other wins were at Bridgehampton,New York, Islip,New York,and Watkins Glen ,New York. This last was the first Grand National race at Watkins Glen since 1957.

A.J. Foyt scored his first Grand National victory by winning the "Firecracker 400" on July 3,1964 at Daytona. This race was held one day before "Fireball" Roberts funeral. Driving a Dodge, Foyt's speed was 151.451 mph. He had been born Anthony Joseph Foyt on January 16, 1935, in Houston,Texas. He began racing motorcycles and midget cars, then moved to the IMCA circuit, and finally graduated to USAC at age 22. He had appeared in the first two NASCAR races at Riverside, and by the time of his win at Daytona he had won the Indy 500 twice.

On June 4, in Spartanburg,South Carolina., Elmo Langley scored the first of his two Grand National wins in a Ford.

Langley, from Charlotte,North Carolina, had raced Modifieds in and out of NASCAR since 1955. For many years he was known to millions of stock car racing fans as the driver of the pace car at almost all Winston Cup events.

Ned Jarrett's final race was at Rockingham on October 30, 1966. Ending his career that day gave him the distinction of being the only driver to retire while a reigning champion of NASCAR's premier division.

On November 9,1813, an army of volunteers under the command of General Andrew Jackson, engaged an army of hostile Creek warriors at a town in Northeast Alabama called Talladega. Situated on the frontier between the Creek and Cherokee nations, Talladega translates roughly to "border town". The battle was a rout, with the Creeks suffering two hundred and ninety-nine dead. More than one hundred and fifty years later Talladega would be the scene of a different kind of battle.

Bill France had chosen Talladega as the sight for his most ambitious endeavor. The Alabama International Motor Speedway was a monstrous 2.66 mile tri-oval with thirty-three degree banking.

As expected, when testing began, the new facility produced mind-boggling speeds. However, the seams in the asphalt, combined with the speed, caused tires to deteriorate and blister within just a few laps. Firestone had recently withdrawn from racing and Goodyear had designed new tires just for Talladega, but they simply were not adequate. This obvious safety concern gave the newly formed PDA a point of contention to which it could attach it's list of demands.

Charlie Glotzbach won the pole with a staggering speed of 199.466 mph. However, after the qualifying sessions, the PDA announced that it would boycott the race. They would find, though, that backing down was simply against Bill France's nature. France announced that if he failed to produce a race, all ticket holders would receive a rain check for Talladega and Daytona. In addition, he said that if the race went on as scheduled, he would run in it himself. In the end, France staged the race as planned on September 14. The field was made up of Grand American cars which had raced the day before, and a few defectors from the PDA. Among these were Bobby Isaac and a relatively unknown North Carolinian named Richard Brickhouse. To allow teams ample opportunity to change tires during the race, caution flags for debris were applied very liberally. After 500 miles, Richard Brickhouse, driving the Dodge that Glotzbach had put on the pole, was shown the checkered flag. His only Grand National win came at a speed of 153.778 mph.

With their resolve broken, the wayward drivers of the PDA dutifully finished the rest of the season.

The end of September,1970 saw two wins by Richard Petty, the first coming at Dover. His next win was in the "Home State 200" in Raleigh,North Carolina, on September 30. It is significant because, after twenty-one years, this was the last Grand National race to be run on a dirt track

In 1972, most of the short tracks were eliminated , as the schedule was pared down to thirty-one races, the same basic configuration it retains today. This was done at the behest of R.J. Reynolds, which was only interested in sponsoring races with the greatest seating capacity or the greatest interest from TV networks. This meant that places such as Asheville, Macon, Hickory, Columbia, Greenville, Oxford, Augusta, Beltsville, and Weaverville would no longer be Winston Cup stops.

A.J. Foyt won his only Daytona 500 in 1972 driving the Wood brothers' Mercury with a speed of 161.550 mph. When the NASCAR series returned to California on March 5, the second Winston Cup race run at Ontario Motor Speedway was won for the second time by A.J. Foyt. It was also Foyt's last NASCAR victory. In a career in which he excelled in almost every form of racing, Foyt included seven Grand National victories.

In 1973, with Trenton, New Jersey, removed from the schedule and Ontario Motor Speedway suffering financial trouble, the Winston Cup season consisted of only twenty-eight races. This was the shortest Grand National schedule since 1950.The new season would be dominated by the same group of drivers which had monopolized the '72 campaign. They would, however, be rejoined in '73 by Cale Yarborough. Yarborough had missed virtually the entire '72 season as he tried his luck on the USAC circuit. When he returned to NASCAR, it was behind the wheel of Junior Johnson's

Chevrolet. By the time their association ended both their names would be etched permanently in the record books.

Only two races were run in August,1973. The first, at Talladega, was won by a virtual unknown named Dick Brooks. Fate contributed to Brooks only Winston Cup win, as most of the big name drivers experienced mechanical problems. Fate was also waiting for Larry Smith, the rookie of the year in '72. Smith came through the tri-oval,slid into the wall in turn one, and was killed instantly.

This incident may explain Bobby Isaac's behavior near the midpoint of the race. Isaac was driving a Ford for Bud Moore when he left turn four, entered pit road, and turned off the car. He climbed out of the car, claiming that he would never race on a super speedway again. He would tell friends that he heard a voice tell him to get out of the car, then later deny having said any such thing. Though he would try to maintain his career, his reputation had been severely damaged.

The 1974 season was one of the most predictable in NASCAR's history. Four drivers, Petty, Pearson, Allison, and Yarborough, would win every race except for one. In fact, parity was unheard of for the entire first half of the decade. Of the 167 top NASCAR division races run from 1971-1976, an astonishing 140 were won by Richard Petty, David Pearson, Bobby Allison, Cale Yarborough, and Buddy baker.

Newcomers and old timers alike would compete for the '75 championship within the confines of a new points system. The new scheme was designed by Bob Latford , the Public Relations Director at Atlanta International Raceway , on the back of a cocktail napkin. Latford's system called for the winning driver to receive 175 points, with the points decreasing by five for each successive top five position. This would make second place worth 170 points,third worth 165, and so on. For positions six through ten the increment was four, so that sixth place was worth 150 points, seventh was worth 146, and so on. For eleventh place to last points would decrease in increments of three. In addition , bonuses of five points would be awarded for leading any one lap and for leading the greatest number of laps in a race. The maximum points possible in a race therefore was 185, which would be awarded if the winning driver had also led the most laps. This system would remain basically in place for thirty-five years..

The 1976 edition of the "World 600" ,which was run on May 30, was notable because it was the first top level NASCAR race to feature a female driver since the days of Sara Christian. Janet Guthrie was an established sports car racer who wanted to race in the '76 edition of the Indianapolis 500. When she failed to qualify, she found herself provided with a $10,000 fee and a stock car, which she did qualify for the "World 600". Some have speculated that Guthrie's appearance was a publicity stunt engineered by Bruton Smith, who had resumed control of Charlotte Motor Speedway after a long exile. Guthrie finished in fifteenth place, twenty-one laps behind David Pearson

The 1977 running of the "600" was the scene of a promotional event gone somewhat awry. "Humpy" Wheeler, General Manager of Charlotte Motor Speedway, had arranged for a Ford to be driven in the "World 600" by Willy T. Ribbs. Ribbs, a road racer from California, would have been the first black driver to appear on the Winston Cup circuit since Wendell Scott had retired several years before. However, when Ribbs failed to appear for a practice session, the offer of the car was withdrawn. The ride went instead to a young driver from nearby Kannapolis, North Carolina, named Dale Earnhardt

In the final weeks of the 1977 Winston Cup campaign, Darrell Waltrip posted two wins to Cale Yarborough's one, but it was too little, too late. By the time Neil Bonnett won the last race at Ontario on November 20, Yarborough had already clinched his second championship. While he did have the most wins, Yarborough's hallmark had been consistency. He managed to finish every race on the schedule, the first time since 1962 that any driver had done so. He finished with 9 victories and an even 5,000 points. He also became the first Winston Cup driver to claim over $500,000 in winnings. The rest of the top ten were Richard Petty, Benny Parsons, Darrell Waltrip, Buddy Baker, Dick Brooks, James Hylton, Bobby Allison, Richard Childress, and Cecil Gordon

While most of the principal players remained the same for the 1978 Winston Cup season, there were a few significant changes. Chief among these was a number of drivers flocking to Oldsmobile, among them defending champion Cale Yarborough. Ford, which had been winless the previous year, and Bobby Allison, who had been winless the previous two, both returned to victory lane in '78. At the other end of the spectrum was Richard Petty. Saddled with the hopeless Dodge Magnum, Petty would go without a victory for the first time in seventeen years.

The last two winners of 1978 were Allisons: Donnie at Atlanta and Bobby at Ontario. The Atlanta race proved to be the scene of tremendous drama and confusion. As the checkered flag was waved the crowd saw a photo finish between Richard Petty and Dave Marcis, with Petty enjoying a one foot advantage. The spectators, thinking they had witnessed the end of Petty's losing streak, were ecstatic. Exuberance turned to bewilderment when Donnie Allison was directed into the winner's circle. After Allison's press conference, it was announced that the scoring cards indicated that the actual winner was Petty, at which point he held a press conference. After hours of review, it was determined that a scorer had failed to give credit for a single lap. Donnie Allison was already at home in Hueytown, Alabama when he received a phone call telling him that the victory was his.

The conviction which stemmed from Junior Johnson being caught at the family still in 1957 was erased in 1986 when Johnson received a pardon from President Ronald Reagan.

Though there have been scoring errors on occasion and penalties within a race are common, on only one occasion has NASCAR actually stripped a driver of a win. It happened at a June 1991 race at Sears Point. As they entered the final turn of the race, the car of Ricky Rudd tapped that of Davey Allison. Allison spun and Rudd passed him for the lead and what he expected would be a checkered flag. Instead,he was shown the black flag. With modern scoring and video tape, there was no question of who was on which lap. Rudd had clearly won the race. NASCAR made the decision, however, to place Rudd in second and award the win, including prizes and points, to Allison.

The distinction for gutsiest driver ever may have to go to Davey Allison .On July 19,1992, Davey was involved in a horrific crash at Pocono, the track which had ended his father's career. Despite a concussion, broken ribs, and a broken right arm, Allison made the start one week later at Talladega. He made an even more courageous display several weeks later at Michigan. With his broken arm attached to the gear shifter with velcro, he took the green flag despite the fact that his brother Clifford had died on the same track just days before.

Like an updated version of Fonty Flock, NASCAR stalwart Dave Marcis competed for virtually his entire career in a pair of wing tipped shoes.

The last driver to lap the entire field in a victory was Geoff Bodine. He accomplished this enviable feat in the Fall of 1994 at North Wilkesboro.

The largest fine ever issued by NASCAR is $200,000. It was assessed in May,2009 against driver Carl Long and his crew chief Charles Swing. The infraction was an oversized engine.

Cale Yarborough and Kyle Busch share the distinction of being the only two drivers to win in NASCAR's top division on their birthdays.

THE ME DECADE

After the twin debacles of Talladega and the PDA in 1969, the new decade started on a more positive note for NASCAR. A deal was reached with ABC which was worth 1.3 million dollars and called for the broadcast of nine races, mostly as part of the network's "Wide World of Sports" series, with some portions broadcast live. This was NASCAR's first significant broadcast arrangement.

In 1970 Richard Petty was involved in a jaw dropping wreck at Darlington. After striking the retaining wall his car was flung a full two stories into the air. When it came to a rest Petty's arm and head were seen dangling out the window. It was after this that NASCAR mandated window netting for the driver's window. Amazingly, this move came six years after the death of Joe Weatherly.

The early Seventies were the career pinnacle for a driver who had struggled longer and harder than possibly anyone else to attain success in the world of stock car racing.

Bobby Isaac was born in 1932 and grew up in a rural area outside of Charlotte. Both of his parents were dead by the time he reached the age of thirteen and he and his eight siblings were left to raise themselves. As a result Isaac had virtually no education. The family subsisted on farming and were so poor that Bobby is alleged to have not owned a pair of shoes until he was sixteen and was in his twenties before his first visit to a restaurant.

Racing proved to be a way out of this lifestyle for Isaac. In 1955 he landed a ride in the Sportsman division and would race on a circuit in the Carolinas at places such as Gaffney, Cowpens, Hickory, and Columbia. By the late 50's he was successful enough to be tapped as a relief driver for several Grand National teams.

He finally scored his own Grand National ride by the early Sixties but met with limited success. The banning of Chrysler's Hemi in 1965 forced Isaac to the USAC circuit where he won two races. Finally, in the late Sixties he landed in the right place. He teamed up with car owner Nord Krauskopf and crew chief Harry Hyde and won three races in 1968. In 1971 this same team would produce eleven wins and secure Isaac's only championship. In 1971 he branched out and set numerous stock car speed records on the Bonneville Salt Flats. He left the Krauskopf team in 1972 with 37 wins. Though he would continue to compete into the late Seventies his career would never again reach such heights.

Though Buddy Baker had made his NASCAR debut back in 1959 his greatest success came in the Seventies. His first two victories were at Charlotte in 1967 and 1968.

Throughout the Seventies he showed a uncanny knack for winning on the biggest stages. Multiple victories would come at Darlington, Charlotte, and Talladega. His greatest triumph was the 1980 Daytona 500 which he won at an astounding average of 177.602 mph. His last victory was in 1983, again at Daytona. When he finally retired in 1993 he had the distinction of having competed in five different decades. His career after he climbed out of his stock car included stints as a television broadcaster.

1971 would bring the most significant changes that NASCAR had seen since it's inception in 1947. Most notably, '71 marked the first full year of the partnership between NASCAR and the R.J. Reynolds Tobacco Company. With cigarette advertisements banned from television, R.J.Reynolds was in search of a new means to keep it's Winston brand of cigarettes and other products in the public eye. Though most of the bootlegger-turned-racer types, such as Tim Flock and Junior Johnson, were gone, the available crop of drivers presented a more than adequate image. Unlike previous sponsors, usually automotive products which promoted a single race, R.J. Reynolds would sponsor the entire series. As such, the official name of NASCAR's elite division became

"Winston Cup Grand Nationals", the champion of which would be awarded the Winston Cup.

The influx of tobacco money, however, would only serve as a band-aid on the wound racing would suffer from the other major development of 1971. This was the sudden and final withdrawal of the factories from stock car racing. The move was spear-headed by Ford, which announced in late 1970 that it would fold all of it's racing operations, maintaining only a small presence in NHRA. As for Chrysler, it ended it's sponsorship of all teams except Petty Enterprises. This was all brought about mostly by a changing economy. Automobile sales were down, and the trend was away from Detroit's big models and towards smaller cars and imports. In addition, the companies had to spend millions to have their factories conform to a spate of recent legislation. Finally, the return on racing programs simply were no longer worth the costs. It is estimated that Ford was spending as much as $30 million annually on race sponsorships. When belts had to be tightened in Detroit, the race programs were the first thing to go.

The unfortunate result was that only the well financed teams could compete. That being the case, the rest of the decade would be almost entirely dominated by four drivers: Richard Petty, David Pearson, Bobby Allison, and Cale Yarborough. Of course there were exceptions, one of which came in the season opener at Riverside. With Dan Gurney retired and Parnelli Jones, along with many NASCAR regulars, staying home, Ford's stranglehold on this track was challenged for the second straight year. The winner, in a Dodge, was Ray Elder, a veteran of the West coast stock car circuit.

In February, Daytona would be the scene of additional change. The 500 was expected to be the first test of an innovation that is still a source of controversy today: the restrictor plate. This is simply a thin metal plate with four holes hole drilled in it, typically 15/16's of an inch in diameter. It is placed between the carburetor and engine, reducing the flow of fuel mixture, thus reducing horsepower and slowing down the car. Originally, plates were intended to increase competition, but today are touted as a means of increasing safety.

In January, Bill France had announced that the plates would be required only on the 426 cubic inch engines. Then, just weeks before Daytona, he dictated that they would also be mandatory on the 366 cubic inch "mini-hemi". As a result, most teams which had been running the 366 simply reverted to the 426. One additional restriction was that any car with a raised spoiler, such as a Superbird or Daytona, would be limited to a 305 cubic inch engine. The twin qualifying races were won by Pete Hamilton in a Plymouth and David Pearson in a Mercury which was powered by a restricted 429 cubic inch engine. The 500 was run on Valentine's Day. A.J. Foyt was leading in the Wood brothers' Mercury, but had to pit for fuel with less than forty laps to go. This left Richard Petty and his teammate, Buddy Baker, to finish first and second. Petty thus became the first three time Daytona 500 winner

One driver who enjoyed his hay day during the '70's was William Caleb "Cale" Yarborough who was born on March 27,

1939, in Timmonsville,South Carolina. By '65 he had been a farmer, semi-pro football player, and modified racer. The tenacity that he would exhibit later in life first became evident when, as a young man, he survived both a lightning strike and a snakebite. In 1963 he was the victor over Benny Parsons in a famous audition which was engineered by Jaque Passino. In late '64 he was given a job as a carpenter at the garage of John Holman and Ralph Moody. When driver Bob Johns departed, the car was placed into Yarborough's hands. He responded with one win and thirty-four top ten finishes.

Another racing superstar who had been on the circuit for years but is most commonly associated with the Seventies is Bobby Allison. He was born Robert Arthur Allison on December 3,1937, in Miami,Florida. He ran his first race while a senior in high school. After graduation, an uncle who worked for Mercury Outboard convinced Karl Kiekhaefer to give Bobby a job testing boat engines. During one such test Allison's boat flipped and he had to be rescued by a nurse who happened to live on the lake. From there he moved up to a mechanic's job with Kiekhaefer's racing operation. When he could no longer resist the racing bug, he moved to Alabama to be at the center of modified racing, a circuit he would soon come to dominate. He made his NASCAR debut in 1961 at the Daytona 500 in a car owned by his brother-in-law,Ralph Stark. Here he finished 31st in a field of 58.The '66 season was his first serious attempt at a Grand National career. At one race, when he felt Curtis Turner had wrecked him unjustly, he sought his revenge on a caution lap and was promptly fined. He finished the year with three victories, all in a Chevrolet

On March 24,1970 Buddy Baker revealed the awesome potential of the still new Alabama International Motor Speedway. Driving a Dodge, Baker became the first driver to break the 200 mph barrier on a closed course. His speed was 200.447 mph

NASCAR made it's debut at a new West coast super speedway, the Ontario Motor Speedway, in the Spring of 1971.The track was an almost exact replica of the Indianapolis Motor Speedway, built near Ontario, California. Scoring his fourth NASCAR victory, A.J.Foyt undoubtedly drew on his Indy experience

On May 9th,1971 at South Boston,Virginia., a newcomer named Benny Parsons won his first Grand National race. Parsons was born July 12,1941. He began his career in the Detroit area, competing on the ARCA circuit. After winning the ARCA championship in '68 and '69, he made the move up to Grand National racing, campaigning in a Ford. In '71 he switched to Mercury, and in his South Boston win he out dueled the likes of Bobby Isaac and Richard Petty. He would score his only championship two years later in 1973 by one of the slimmest margins ever. Benny Parsons points total was

7173.80, followed by Cale Yarborough with 7106. 65. Though he had only one victory, Parsons had twenty-one top ten finishes, more than any other driver. He would go on to win the 1975 Daytona 500 and finished his career with twenty-one victories. After his retirement Parsons was a popular commentator during race telecasts for many years before he passed away in 2007.

In 1972, most of the short tracks were eliminated , as the schedule was pared down to thirty-one races. Though there have been numerous changes since, the schedule is only slightly longer today. This was done at the behest of R.J. Reynolds, which was only interested in sponsoring races with the greatest seating capacity or the greatest interest from TV networks. This meant that places such as Ashville, Macon, Hickory, Columbia, Greenville, Oxford, Augusta, Beltsville, and Weaverville would no longer be Winston Cup stops.

A more significant change came behind the scenes, as NASCAR's president, Bill France, retired. The reigns were handed over to his son, William C. France, also known as Bill France, Jr. Billy, as he was often called, once tried to drive but quickly found that he preferred the operational side of racing. He worked his way up to NASCAR vice-president, where he was responsible for decisions on starts, postponements, and cautions, among other things. When Bill France stepped down from NASCAR, he remained as head of the corporation which ran Daytona and Talladega, and he also played an instrumental role in Alabama Governor George Walace's 1972 bid for the White House.

Though he barely had one third of his victories from the year before, Richard Petty still emerged as champion in 1972 with 8701.40 points. However, he had to settle for second place in terms of money won, as top honors went to Bobby Allison. Petty probably didn't mind, as he had become NASCAR's first four time champion. This particular feat of Petty's would not be equaled for more than fifteen years. The rest of the top ten in '72 were James Hylton, Cecil Gordon, Benny Parsons, Walter Ballard, Elmo Langley, John Sears, Dean Dalton, and Ben Arnold.

The first race of '73, the "Winston Western 500", saw two new names in victory lane:Mark Donahue and Matador. To say that either one had a fleeting impact on stock car racing would be an overstatement. The opposite is true, however, of the man who owned the car, Roger Penske. Penske was a native of Ohio who came from a fairly prosperous family. He began racing sports cars while a student at Lehigh University in Pennsylvania. During this period he met Donahue and the two soon formed a racing team. They began with Can-Am and SCCA racing, and in 1969, when they made their first foray into USAC, Donahue was rookie of the year at Indianapolis. Penske parleyed their racing success into a small empire by starting a truck leasing company and acquiring car dealerships. In '72 the team won the Trans-Am title with an AMC Javelin and in '72 Donahue won the Indianapolis 500. They also ran AMC's Matador on the Winston Cup circuit for the first time in '72. While the '73 Riverside victory was the only NASCAR win for Donahue, it would not be the last for Matador and certainly not for Penske.

Richard Petty would etch his name in the record book yet again in 1974 by being NASCAR's first winner at a new venue: the Pocono International Raceway, located near Long Pond, Pennsylvania. Pocono is like many other tracks in that it is 2.5 miles long. However, the track's configuration redefines the term "tri-oval". This is because it has only three sides and three turns. The turns are of three different degrees and each is banked at a slightly different angle. The track was built by a group called Racing Incorporated, which was formed in 1957. The 1,025 acre site, most of which had been a spinach farm, was purchased in 1962. Racing Incorporated, headed by Dr. Joe Mattioli and David Montgomery, raised about $4 million through a stock sale and broke ground in 1965.A prominent feature of the track would be it's 3,740 foot long front straightaway, which today is the longest in NASCAR. A 3/4 mile oval was built which incorporated part of this straightaway, and it was on this oval that Pocono's first race was run. The event took place on May 4,1969, but was marred by the death of a young driver named Troy Ruttman,Jr. By 1971 the track was completed, and a 500 mile Indy-car race was held on July 3. Later the same year the track hosted a USAC stock car race, but it would be another three years before Pocono saw a Winston Cup event. That first 500 mile race was shortened due to rain, and Richard Petty's average speed was only 115.593 mph.

On May 10,1975 a newcomer would win a Winston Cup race for the first time since Earl Ross' victory at Martinsville the previous September. However, this driver would prove to have considerably more staying power than Ross. Darrell Waltrip first appeared in a Winston Cup winner's circle at a 250 mile race in Nashville, Tennessee. Experience no doubt contributed to his victory, as Waltrip had competed at Nashville for years in Sportsman races. He had been born February 5, 1947, near Owensboro,Kentucky. His grandmother took him to his first dirt track race, and he began a prolific go-kart career while in his early teens. During high school he was a track and basketball standout.

After graduation he bought a used race car and began to dominate the local dirt tracks. He soon got the opportunity to drive a top notch late model Chevelle, with the stipulation that he move to Franklin,Tennessee. Waltrip made the move, and in 1971 won eleven late model events at Nashville. He made his first foray into Winston Cup racing in 1972 then, late in the '73 season, moved to Bud Moore's Ford. However, he was replaced for the '74 campaign and was forced to form his own Chevrolet team. He kept finishing higher and higher, until he broke through at Nashville, where he finished two laps ahead of the field.

Another first timer would make his way to victory lane in 1975 at a September race in Martinsville. Dave Marcis had been born March 1,1941, in Wuasau, Wisconsin. In the early stages of his career he won a state championship in Wisconsin, along with USAC and NASCAR late model races. He began racing as an independent on the Grand National circuit in 1968. His break came late in '75 when he was offered the #71 K&K Insurance Dodge, the same car which had recently been occupied by Bobby Isaac and Buddy Baker. The car's owners had withheld the team from the '74 season to protest NASCAR's restrictions on the big block engines, but returned in '75 with Marcis as the new driver. Though not a household name, Marcis is one of NASCAR's most enduring drivers, having competed in four different decades.

In 1975, after reacquiring stock for years, Bruton Smith became majority shareholder in the Charlotte Motor Speedway. He immediately set about a years long series of improvements to the track, and today it is without question one of the premier facilities in all of sports.

The 1976 season would place no new names in the winner's circle, but it would produce a first time champion. The season began as it had many times before,with the Wood brothers' driver, in this case David Pearson, capturing the checkered flag at Riverside.

Victory number two for Pearson would come quickly, but not easily. From it's inauguration Daytona International Speedway was the scene of highly dramatic finishes. The '76 edition of the 500 would continue the tradition. The duel between Richard Petty and David Pearson in the '76 "Daytona 500" may always be regarded as the most exciting and memorable finish in NASCAR's history.

News was made at the speedway even before the green flag fell. The top three qualifiers, A.J. Foyt, Darrell Waltrip, and Dave Marcis, all recorded speeds in excess of 185 mph. However, all three efforts were promptly disallowed. In the case of Foyt and Waltrip, their vehicles were discovered to have nitrous oxide kits, designed to deliver a boost in horsepower. Marcis' car had a flap on the radiator which blocked the airflow, allowing the engine to warm up faster. All three re-qualified, with Foyt still running the fastest overall lap. However, the rules dictated that he start back in the field.

The actual race was quickly distilled to just two elements, Petty and Pearson. Towards the end of the event they were the only drivers on the lead lap, with Benny Parsons in third place, one lap down. On the final lap , Pearson passed Petty on the backstretch for the lead. Petty tried to regain the lead in turn three but failed to do so. Undeterred, he moved to Pearson's inside again in turn four. He had almost completed the pass when his Dodge became loose and tapped the front left of Pearson's Mercury. What ensued was nothing short of mayhem. Both cars skidded out of control and hit the outside wall, then bounced back towards the infield. Pearson slid onto the pit road entrance and was clipped by a car driven by Joe Frasson. Petty slid down the track and stopped on the infield grass. Both cars were stalled and had extensive front end damage. However, Pearson was able to re-fire his engine, while Petty was not. Pearson coaxed his Mercury slowly across the grass and back onto the track. As he did so, Parsons flew past him, putting himself back on the lead lap. Pearson then crossed the finish line, taking the checkered flag at about 20 mph. In the meantime, some crewmen had crossed the pit wall and were pushing Petty's car. This resulted in an automatic one lap penalty, but Petty was still credited with second place, while Parsons remained in third. Pearson took a slow victory lap then turned down pit road. Here, Petty approached the damaged Mercury, stuck his head in the window, and apologized for the incident. Pearson could probably not have been more grateful. Though he had dominated all the super speedways for years, he had never won the "Daytona 500". It would be his only win in the famed event.

By teaming with Junior Johnson in 1976, Cale Yarborough would realize an achievement that could not be claimed by Petty,Pearson, or any other driver for decades to come.

In their first year together Yarborough was absolutely dominant on the short tracks. He threw in a July Daytona win for good measure and notched his first title by a margin of almost 200 points.

In 1977 it was Darrell Waltrip, not David Pearson, who would be the most consistent challenger for Yarborough. Their feud spilled from the track and into the press, with Yarborough famously giving Waltrip the nickname "Jaws". Ultimately, Yarborough got the last laugh in the form of his second title.

In the final weeks of the 1978 season , Yarborough went on a late season tear, winning races at Bristol, Martinsville, North Wilkesboro , and Rockingham. To these victories he added his fourth win in the "Southern 500" on September 4.

Cale Yarborough's points lead was so large that Bobby Allison's win in the final race at Ontario did not even dent it. Yarborough's 4,841 points put him almost 500 ahead of the second place Allison. He also had 10 wins and 24 top ten finishes. After Allison the rest of the top ten were Darrell Waltrip, Benny Parsons, Dave Marcis, Richard Petty, Lennie Pond, Dick Brooks, Buddy Arrington, and Richard Childress.

For many,many years it seemed as though Yarborough would be the only driver to win three consecutive Cup championships. He will, at least, always be the first.

On February 11,1979, Kyle Petty made his racing debut in an ARCA race at Daytona. The eighteen year old qualified second, and with seemingly no effort won the event.

The 1979 season began with Darrell Waltrip's first victory at Riverside. Over the next few years he would dominate the road course as only Dan Gurney and Richard Petty had before. When the series moved to Daytona in February, the result was yet another wild finish. That Richard Petty won a record sixth "Daytona 500" was about the only normal occurrence. Petty set the new mark in his second new make in as many years, having switched from Chevrolet to Oldsmobile. Also, CBS made the race the first 500 mile event to be broadcast live in it's entirety.

The television audience would be treated to some of the best driving that NASCAR had to offer, though not necessarily the best behavior. In the early stages of the race Donnie Allison lost control of his car in the backstretch. This forced his brother Bobby and Cale Yarborough to go sliding through the sand and water which had collected on the infield. The moisture prevented Yarborough from re-firing his car. By the time he did so he was four laps down.

However, through shear will and some timely caution flags, Yarborough erased the deficit. As the race drew to a close Donnie Allison and Yarborough were running first and second. As they charged down the backstretch for the last time, Yarborough tried to pass Allison on his inside. However, Allison tried to block the move and forced Yarborough onto the grass. As Yarborough fought his way back onto the track, Allison was sent sliding into the outside wall while Yarborough crashed in the infield. Petty, Darrell Waltrip, and A.J. Foyt, who had been fighting for third place about one half lap behind, then raced past the disabled pair. Waltrip made a last desperate bid to pass Petty, but came up just inches short. Petty had run the race against the advise of his doctor, as he was still recovering from off-season surgery in which part of his stomach was removed.

The excitement was just beginning, however. As the checkered flag was waving, Yarborough exited his Oldsmobile, strode up to Allison's Chevrolet, and punched him while he was still behind the wheel. Before Donnie could retaliate, his brother Bobby pulled up, jumped out of his Ford, and intervened on Donnie's behalf. He punched Yarborough then threw him to the ground. The melee that ensued became so pitched that the drivers' helmets were used as weapons. Not to be outdone, the drivers' crews initiated a brawl of their own on pit road. Yarborough would later claim that Bobby Allison was using his lapped vehicle to block him, even timing his pit stops so as to stay between Yarborough and Donnie Allison. Allison, of course, denied any wrong doing. While these outbursts were not uncommon in racing, they were rarely on such a scale or on live national television.

Most of the '79 season was dominated by Darrell Waltrip, as he scored victories at Darlington, Charlotte, Texas, Nashville, Talladega, and Bristol. Down the home stretch, however, he seemed unable to handle the pressure as he suffered a series of poor finishes and black flags.

When the series reached the final race at Ontario, Waltrip's lead was barely discernible at only two points. Richard Petty led the race early, thus picking up five bonus points and taking the points lead. However, Waltrip erased that advantage when he took the lead on the ninth lap. After that, slow pit stops and near collisions put Waltrip one lap down. While Benny Parsons won the race, Petty won his final title by finishing fifth to Waltrip's eighth. It was a record seventh championship for Petty, which at the time seemed unmatchable. It was also the tightest points race to that point, with Petty's 4,830 points placing him just eleven ahead of Waltrip. The rest of the top ten were Bobby Allison, Cale Yarborough, Benny Parsons, Joe Millikan, Dale Earnhardt, Richard Childress,Ricky Rudd, and Terry Labonte.

DANCING WITH MR D

Perhaps the definitive example of a pre-World War II stock car racer is the tragic figure of Lloyd Seay. Before his demise at the age of twenty-one, Seay was one of the most notorious liquor haulers and dirt track racers in and around Atlanta. He was a native of Dawson County, Georgia, who in just the final year of his life won races at Allentown Pennsylvania, Greensboro, North Carolina, Highpoint, North Carolina, and Daytona.

His Daytona victory came on August 21, 1941.He started fifteenth but was soon in the lead and dominated the event on his way to the checkered flag. It was during this race that a photographer captured an iconic picture of Seay barreling though one of the turns with his machine's two left wheels up in the air.

On September 1,1941,he was entered in a race at Lakewood Speedway,where he had also won previously. He had missed qualifying and so had to start at the rear of the field. Also,for unknown reasons he had changed his usual number 7 to 13 that day. However, his luck was apparently unaffected. Seay was first to the checkered flag, followed by Bill Dawson,Skimp Hersey,Jake Howard,and Wilbur Cavender.

It was not until the next day that Seay's good fortune abandoned him. On September 2, Lloyd and his brother Robert were at the home of a cousin named Grover Anderson,in Dahlonega,Georgia. A dispute erupted, apparently over a load of sugar. Lloyd was shot and killed and his brother was wounded. Anderson,along with his son Woodrow,was arrested for the murder. In the months counting down to Pearl Harbor, few people probably realized that an era died along with Lloyd Seay.

John "Skimp" Hersey was a native of Saint Augustine, Florida who competed in NASCAR's first Grand National race. It was also the last time he competed at the top level as he was severely burned at Lakewood Park Speedway during a race in June of 1950. After his brakes failed Hersey's car flipped. He escaped from the vehicle but emerged into a gasoline inferno, a horrifying scene which was captured by newspaper photographers. Hersey died the next day.

Another shocking scene occurred at a NASCAR sponsored Modified race at Raleigh in 1953. The car driven by Bill Blevins stalled on the backstretch during the final pace lap. The flagman failed to notice, however, and sent the field of fifty-nine cars speeding into the helpless Blevins. An enormous crash, followed by a giant fireball, were all but inevitable. Both Blevins and Jesse Midkiff died in the fifteen car disaster.

Buddy Shuman was a native of Charlotte who drove for a plethora of owners in the late '40's and '50's. He was also known to haul liquor and had once survived a gunshot wound to the neck during one of his runs. His lone Grand National victory came at Stamford Park Race Track in Canada during the 1952 campaign. Only seventeen cars entered this race and only six were running at it's conclusion. Shuman died in a hotel fire in Hickory, North Carolina on November 13,1955. A charred mattress indicated a smoking accident. In the confusion Shuman had torn down the bathroom door in a vain attempt to escape the smoke In his honor NASCAR renamed what had been it's Lifetime Achievement Award as the Buddy Shuman Award.

Considering that the machines that made up the field in NASCAR's early years truly were stock cars, it is amazing that there were not more fatalities in these formative days. However, the karmic wheel keeps on turning and the good luck was bound to run out someday. Not surprisingly, it ran out at Darlington. At the 1957 version of the Southern 500 Fonty Flock spun out and came to a stop against the retaining wall. In the days before spotters there was no warning for Bobby Myers, who came flying around the track and struck the stationary vehicle. His car was flipped into the air, disintegrating as it went. Flock survived but his career was over. Myers was dead at the scene. Early during the next season, his brother Billy also met an untimely end. While racing at Bowman-Gray Stadium in Winston-Salem,North

Carolina, Billy Myers pulled his car off the track and turned off the engine. When track officials arrived they found him dead of a heart attack.

Gwyn Staley was a winner of several early Grand National events and had helped his brother Enoch build the North Wilkesboro speedway. He was killed in a convertible race at Richmond in 1958.

On September 21,1958, disaster would strike Junior Johnson yet again. On a Sunday when a Martinsville race had been rained out, Johnson was out collecting some old debts. After he fell asleep at the wheel, his Plymouth ran through the stop sign at the intersection of North Carolina 39 and U.S. 64, striking another vehicle. A passenger in the other car, Viola Sanders, was critically wounded and died the next day. On the same day that Johnson attended her funeral, his home was raided and his father and brother were arrested. Johnson and his mother surrendered to police the following day. Though Johnson was acquitted in the case against his family, he would eventually plead no contest to manslaughter charges.

On February 11,1959 the career of Marshall Teague came to an untimely end. He was performing a test at the just opened Daytona International Speedway in an open wheeled car that was intended to compete on the USAC circuit later that year. Teague lost control of the car in turn three and the seat, driver included, was flung from the vehicle. Teague was killed instantly.

The novelty of Wendall Scott's lone victory would be over-shadowed on January 19,1964, at Riverside. This was the date of the second annual Grand National race at the California road course. Among the NASCAR regulars who made the trek West was Joe Weatherly. "Little Joe" was notoriously superstitious. Because a wreck in which a close friend was killed had occurred in a green Buick, he could not stand to see anything green in the pits. He had a similar phobia of peanuts. He was no doubt somewhat wary of the fact that the flight that brought him to California was number 13. Once at the track his qualifying effort put him in the thirteenth starting position. When the race started it appeared that Richard Petty had the strongest car, but mechanical problems sent him to the garage. Weatherly's luck had also deteriorated as a long pit stop left him well off the pace. On lap 113 his luck ran out completely. When entering turn 6, one of the few right hand turns in all of NASCAR, Weatherly lost control and crashed into the retaining wall that bordered the track. His safety harness is thought to have been lose, but it may not have mattered. Though he was only going about sixty mph, the force of the crash snapped his head through the open driver's window and into the wall. He was killed instantly. Afterward, an examination of his personal effects revealed that he had thirteen dollars in his wallet. Joe Weatherly was respected and well liked by his fellow drivers, and his death cast an ominous pall over all of them. It was the first time that a reigning NASCAR champion had been lost in a fatal accident, but sadly, it would not be the last.

Tragedy would strike again in 1964 when the "World 600", was run at Charlotte. Almost exactly four months after Joe Weatherly's death another NASCAR great would be struck down.

The Charlotte Motor Speedway had never been kind to "Fireball" Roberts. Though he had several good qualifying efforts and several second place finishes at the track, he had no wins. It was one of the few regular NASCAR tracks on which he had no career victories. He had also been involved in a horrendous wreck at Charlotte in 1961, when his Pontiac was T-boned by the Ford of Bill Morgan. On that occasion he would walk away from the crash, something he would not do on May 24, 1964.

In the early stages of the "600", the leaders were Ned Jarrett, Junior Johnson, and Roberts, all three in Fords, and Darrell Dieringer in a Mercury. As Johnson tried to pass Jarrett in turn two, their cars made contact and began to spin. Behind them, Roberts also spun, while Dieringer somehow made it through the mayhem. Jarrett and Roberts both hit the inside retaining wall and both their cars burst into flames, with Roberts' car on it's roof. Jarrett leaped from his car and rushed to the aid of his fellow driver. Jarrett pulled Roberts from the flaming wreckage, and together they tore off his burning jumpsuit.

With first and second degree burns on over 70% of his body, Roberts was flown to Charlotte Memorial Hospital. Jim Paschal would eventually win the race, but that seemed almost trivial. The hospital issued a plea for blood to supply the 123 pints that Roberts would require over the next three days. After five days he was removed from intensive care and placed under heavy sedation. His arms, legs, and back were severely burned, though his face was undamaged. In a couple of weeks it became necessary to amputate the fingers of one hand.

During this time he asked about the results of the Indianapolis 500. He was told that A.J. Foyt had won, but his doctors declined to mention that two other drivers, Eddie Sachs and Dave MacDonald, had been killed. In late June he developed septicemia and pneumonia, then lapsed into a coma. At 7:15 a.m. on July 2,1964, one of NASCAR's first and brightest stars was gone. His last victory had come on November 17, 1963, in Augusta,Georgia. In his Grand National career he crossed the finish line first thirty-three times.

In September of 1964 tire tests would claim another victim. Jimmy Pardue was a veteran who had won twice on the Grand National circuit. During a test at Charlotte on September 22 a blown tire sent him through the guardrail and to his doom. Incredibly, he still finished fifth in points that year.

When racing resumed in 1965 the cars would all be equipped with a new safety feature. After the death of "Fireball" Roberts, the stock gas tank was replaced by a "fuel cell", which had been developed by Firestone. A series of baffles and a sponge-like bladder inside this cell help to diminish the possibility of gas spilling after a wreck. Also, a driver's window net, which Lee Petty had used for several years, was becoming commonplace.

These innovations were not enough to save Billy Wade,

however. Wade was killed in a crash at Daytona on January 5 during a test session for Goodyear. Darrell Dieringer was part of the same test program and had crashed a week earlier,escaping with a broken collar bone and broken ribs. Wade would not be so fortunate. He was on the track alone when one of his tires blew. The right side of his Mercury hit the retaining wall that had been built after Lee Petty and Johhny Beauchamp had flown off the track. When rescue workers reached Wade they found him dead behind the wheel. Wade fared just slightly better than Larry Thomas, who never made it to Daytona. Thomas was killed on January 25, 1965 when he rear-ended another car on a fog bound highway near Tifton,Georgia. Wade and Thomas had their best years in '64, when both men finished in the top ten.

On February 28,1965, Richard Petty's drag racing career took a sudden, tragic turn. Petty was racing his Plymouth Barracuda before a crowd of 12,000 in Dallas,Georgia. Just as Petty left the line on his second run of the day, a tie rod broke on the car, and a wheel was sent flying into the crowd where it struck a small boy. The car itself swerved into a ditch then flew through the air and into the horrified spectators.

While Petty was unhurt, six onlookers were injured. Worst of all, the young boy struck by the wheel, eight year old Wayne Dye of Austell, Georgia, was killed.

The end of September,1970, saw two wins by Richard Petty, the first coming at Dover. His next win was in the "Home State 200" in Raleigh,North Carolina, on September 30.

It is significant because, after twenty-one years, this was the last Grand National race to be run on a dirt track. It is no small irony that, less than a week later, Curtis Turner was dead. Turner had used a private plane for years to commute between races and to evaluate timber land. In typical fashion, he had once landed it on the back stretch at Darlington in order to meet a dare. His passenger on October 5 was a golf pro named Clarence King, who had a history of heart trouble. Turner had a habit of napping in the back of the plane, leaving whoever was aboard at the controls. Some have theorized that King was piloting the plane and that he suffered a heart attack. Both men where killed when the plane crashed into a mountain near Punxsutawney,Pennsylvania. Though he continued to race intermittently, Turner had not won since his Rockingham victory in 1965.

Only two races were run in August,1973. The first, at Talladega, was won by a virtual unknown named Dick Brooks. Fate contributed to Brooks' only Winston Cup win, as most of the big name drivers experienced mechanical problems. Fate was also waiting for Larry Smith, the rookie of the year in '72. Smith came through the tri-oval,slid into the wall in turn one, and was killed instantly.

On May 3,1975, Talladega was the scene of Buddy Baker's first victory since 1973. Baker won the "Winston 500" in a Ford with a speed of 144.948 mph. This raced was marred, however, by the death of Randy Owens, a member of Richard Petty's crew. Owens was family, as was most of Petty's crew, in that he was Petty's brother- in-law. While attempting to douse a grease fire on the #43 Dodge, Owens was thrown two stories into the air when an air compressor exploded. With injuries that included a broken neck, Owens was dead when he hit the ground.

On August 17,1975, history would repeat itself at Talladega. This was good news for Buddy Baker, who won his second race of the year and his second in a row at the monstrous Alabama super-speedway. The news was not so good, however, for Tiny Lund. Lund had been a Grand National fixture since the dirt track days of the nineteen fifties, but his career and life would end on the high banks of Talladega. Lund lost control on the eighth lap of the race and was hit in the side by a car driven by Terry Link. He suffered massive internal injuries and died as a result. He had a total of five Grand National victories, the last of which came in 1971 at North Wilkesboro, North Carolina.

By 1977 Bobby Isaac's Winston Cup career was over. On August 13 he was competing in a late model race at Hickory, North Carolina, when he was overcome by the heat and parked his car with twenty-five laps to go. Whether the cause was the heat or the cumulative effects of his unimaginably hard life, Isaac was suffering a heart attack. He was admitted to a nearby hospital where he died at the age of forty-five.

Lee Roy Yarbrough was another of racing's tragic figures.

He was born in Jacksonville,Florida in 1938 and was racing on the local dirt tracks by his teens. By the early Sixties he was a dominant force in the Sportsman and Modified divisions and began making forays into Grand National events. He found success at the top level in 1964 with wins at Savannah,Georgia and Greenville, South Carolina. In 1966 he added a super speedway win at Charlotte to his resume.

However, during these years he was building a reputation for something other than driving ability. Yarbrough was also notoriously temperamental and violent. This meant that he never stayed with one team for long and even left stock cars on occasion for attempts to run the Indianapolis 500. By the late Sixties he was teamed with Junior Johnson and like many other drivers found his greatest success with the legendary owner. 1969 was by far the pinnacle of his career as he won the Daytona 500 as well as two races each at Darlington and Atlanta.

In 1970 he sustained a head injury during a tire test at Texas World Speedway. The following year he was in another severe crash while practicing for the Indianapolis 500. These injuries seemed to make his behavior more erratic. His last race of any kind came at Martinsville in 1972. He was arrested several times in the late 70's for violent outbursts. These culminated in an attack on his mother in 1980. He was arrested and ultimately found unfit for trial. He would spend the rest of his life in mental institutions. In early December of 1984 he fell while suffering some sort of seizure and struck his head. He was taken to a hospital in Jacksonville where he died from brain injuries the next day.

While battle for the 1989 title raged on the track, the struggle was ending for one driver off the track. After his awe inspiring comeback in 1987, Tim Richmond's condition had deteriorated once again. His appearance became so alarming that some drivers complained to NASCAR. The last straw came at Michigan, where he had to be driven to his pit in a golf cart and placed in his race car. Forced to undergo a drug screening, he failed initially but passed a second test. Never the less, NASCAR insisted that he release his medical records,which Richmond refused to do. This led to his 1988 suspension, from which he never returned. By the summer of '89 he had checked into Good Samaritan Hospital in West Palm Beach, Florida. Only his family and a few friends knew that his bout with pneumonia had been caused by a full blown case of AIDS. This news would cause no small concern in the garage area. While certain aspects of Richmond's persona were contrived, his reputation for hard living was well deserved. However, all who knew him agreed that he was neither gay nor an intravenous drug user. This meant that Richmond had probably contracted the disease from one of the women who followed the Winston Cup circuit, and raised the possibility that he was not the only one infected. He died in West Palm Beach on August 13, 1989.

Just as the 1990 campaign reached its final months, Winston Cup racing was dealt another tragedy. In the North Wilkesboro race which Mark Martin had won on September 30 , the 21st place finisher was Rob Moroso , a twenty-two year old native of Madison ,Connecticutt. The Moroso name had been well known in racing for years. This was because Rob's father, Dick, owned a company which made various auto parts and trailers. He was also the owner of Rob's Winston Cup car.

Moroso had been one of the youngest drivers to ever win a Busch series race and in 1989 became the youngest ever Busch champion. Near midnight after the North Wilkesboro race , Moroso lost control of his Oldsmobile on state highway 150 , near Mooresville, North Carolina. When he crossed into the opposite lane his car was struck on the driver's side by another vehicle. Both Moroso and Tammy Williams, the driver of the other car , were killed instantly. Though he missed the final month of the season , Moroso was still able to win the 1990 Rookie of the Year award.

The Watkins Glen race in August 1991 would prove to be the last for J.D. McDuffie. McDuffie was an independent driver whose modest budget dictated that he race with used and second hand parts. It may have been inferior parts that caused him to lose a tire on the fourth lap. McDuffie slid through a small patch of grass on the road course, hit a retaining wall, and flipped upside down. The car came to rest on a guardrail and McDuffie was killed instantly.

Though the next race was at Pocono, the attention of the racing world shifted suddenly to Talladega in the summer of 1993. The giant super speedway in Alabama was to be the scene of Neil Bonnett's return to racing. In 1992 Bonnett had taken part in a race simulation with Dale Earnhardt, but afterward became dizzy and felt he was not able to handle an actual race. They repeated the test in '93, and this time Bonnett felt he was ready. At Talladega, he was to be Earnhardt's teammate, driving a #31 Chevrolet for Richard Childress. In addition, Bonnett's son David was preparing to make his Busch Grand National debut, also at Talladega.

It was a test session by David Bonnett that lured Davey Allison to Talladega on July 12.Allison was eager to lend support to a fellow member of the "Alabama Gang". That afternoon he and Red Farmer had lunch in Allison's home town of Hueytown, Alabama. Farmer, a veteran of Alabama's dirt tracks, was a longtime associate of the Allison's and crew chief for Davey's Grand National team. After lunch the pair boarded a Hughes 369HS helicopter, which Davey had bought just weeks before, for the thirty minute trip to Talladega. With Allison at the controls they attempted to land in the infield, but disaster struck just one foot from the ground.

Witnesses said the aircraft began to rock back and forth, shot twenty-five feet into the air, spun counterclockwise,tilted to one side, then plummeted to the ground. It landed squarely on the pilot's side, then the still churning rotors caused it to flip onto the passenger side. One of the first people to rush to the scene was Neil Bonnett..

Both men were rushed to Carraway Methodist Medical Center in Birmingham, Alabama, where emergency surgery was performed on Allison. He had suffered a broken pelvis and a punctured lung, but it was the injury to his head that was the most severe. The diagnosis was subdural hematoma, or swelling and bleeding of the brain. Farmer had suffered a broken nose, broken ribs, broken collarbone, broken shoulder, and punctured lung. After a brief stay in intensive care his condition was upgraded to stable.

Throughout that Monday night Allison seemed to be responsive to his doctors and family. However, towards dawn his condition worsened and he was pronounced dead at 8 a.m. Similar to the death of "Fireball" Roberts three decades before, Allison's death robbed NASCAR of one of it's most beloved figures. Just how immensely popular he was became evident during the nationwide outpouring of grief which followed his death.

Neil Bonnett , looking to continue the comeback he started at Talladega, was going to run a limited schedule in '94. Daytona was added to that schedule when Bonnett reached a sponsorship agreement with Country Time Lemonade. On February 11, just moments into a practice session, his Chevrolet slid across the track and into the turn four wall. Bonnett sustained massive head injuries and was dead within thirty minutes. His total career wins numbered eighteen. Another driver looking for his first win was Rodney Orr. Orr was a rookie who had won the Goody's Dash Series championship the previous year. On February 14, the first official day of practice, Orr was also killed in a crash.

Though conditions during the week were exceptionally windy, many felt that these and other crashes were due to the tire companies placing speed ahead of safety. The tension was eased when Hoosier withdrew from the Daytona race, pledging to return later in the season. However, this was after another rookie, Loy Allen, Jr., had driven to the pole on a set of Hoosiers.

Over the decades the various sanctioning bodies have suffered the loss of favorite sons, superstars, and reigning champions. A death that would occur on February 18,2001, however, would shake the stock car world to it's very core.

After almost thirty years there was little that Dale Earnhardt had not accomplished in NASCAR. He had tied the legendary Richard Petty with seven championships. He had won the Daytona 500 in 1998. He had amassed enough winnings to launch his own successful team. He was an innovator at branding himself and marketing his own image,even appearing on QVC and a 2000 Forbes list of richest athletes. In short, had attained the status of icon-a true living legend.

Despite all the success, Earnhardt was never one to rest on his laurels. He had finished second in the points in 2000, and an eighth championship was certainly a feather he would have loved to add to his cap. When the green flag waved at the 2001 Daytona 500 he was still as competitive as ever.

He had plenty of compatriots on the track. Starting with a team on NASCAR's truck series, Earnhardt had expanded the operation to include a Busch series team and eventually two cars on the Winston Cup circuit. These machines were piloted by Michael Waltrip, who had never won a points event, and Earnhardt's son, Dale,Jr.

In addition to the other competitors, each driver was contending with new rules governing the plate and spoiler.

NASCAR is perpetually tinkering with these parameters in the four races that take place each year at Daytona and Talladega. The goal is to keep the speeds under 200 m.p.h. without diminishing the quality of the racing. At the Talladega race the preceding fall, they had hit upon a package they liked and it was still in place for the 500.

The rules changes seemed effective as the more competitive type of racing would eventually result in 49 lead changes. It would also result in "the big one", the massive, field destroying type of wreck that is almost common place at plate races. It came with twenty-seven laps to go and involved nineteen cars. Among the drivers involved was Tony Stewart, whose machine was launched into the air and sent on a breathtaking pinball ride atop the other cars.

The race had to be red-flagged to clean up all the debris, and after being restarted it wound down quickly to it's stunning conclusion. On the white flag lap Dale,Jr. and Michael Waltrip were battling for the lead with the elder Earnhardt right behind them. Some have speculated that Earnhardt was trying to block the rest of the field to preserve the win for one of his teams. Whatever the cause, there was contact between the cars of Sterling Marlin and Earnhardt. This sent the black number 3 into the turn four wall where it was t-boned by the machine of Kenny Schrader. Just seconds later Michael Waltrip would fly across the finish line for the first points victory of his career.

Behind him Earnhardt and Schrader would slide in tandem down the famous Daytona banking and come to rest in the infield. Schrader would climb from his machine and approach Earnhardt's driver side window, then immediately signal for the safety crew. In the television booth an exultant Darrell Waltrip could not relish his brother's triumph for long. The camera caught him gazing toward turn 4 and thinking out loud "Boy, I hope Dale's OK".

The telecast of the race was a benchmark in itself. After decades of individual track owners striking deals with various networks, NASCAR had negotiated a massive contract on behalf of all the tracks with the Fox network and NBC. For whatever reason, the Fox broadcast of the 500 ended awkwardly and abruptly. It would be several hours later that Mike Helton , President of NASCAR, would appear before the press. A visibly shaken Helton announced what many had already concluded: "We've lost Dale Earnhardt".

As had often been the case in the past, the accident resulted in safety improvements, in this case a whole bevy of them. The most well known was the HANS device which helped to reduce whiplash effect to a driver in the case of sudden impact. It had been used on other racing circuits for several years, but in the wake of Earnhardt's death NASCAR made it mandatory. Safer barriers are additions to concrete walls that are intended to dissipate energy. They were already in place in a few tracks but would soon become omnipresent.

NASCAR would also launch a years long redesign of the car bodies. This would eventually result in the COT, or Car of Tomorrow. This design featured more headroom and stiffer bracing and foam padding in the sides of the vehicles. To the dismay of many purists, it also mandated a common body style for all manufacturers.

Dale Earnhardt suffered a basal skull fracture and in all likelihood he died immediately. Like the Beatles or James Dean the public would never see him as a has been, never see him when he wasn't at the top of his game. While icon and legend were appellations he had already earned in life, on a February afternoon in Daytona he became absolutely immortal.

Latter Days

As the Eighties dawned NASCAR's old guard, the Petty-Pearson generation, would find itself in decline. The vacuum had to be filled, and the driver who was best positioned to do so was Darrell Waltrip.

Waltrip had established himself as a consistent winner during the late Seventies driving for the DiGard team. However, to rise to the pinnacle of stock car racing a change in teams would be necessary. Surprisingly, it was his fiercest on track rival, Cale Yarborough, who would provide him the opportunity. Yarborough was harboring plans to run a limited schedule, thus vacating Junior Johnson's car. The most coveted ride in NASCAR would be available, and the first person Yarborough let know was Darrell Waltrip.

The pairing with Johnson was an immediate success, as Waltrip won twenty-four races, twenty-eight poles, and two Winston Cup titles in 1981 and '82. The gravy train came to a screeching halt at the 1983 Daytona 500, however. In the early stages of the race Waltrip suffered one of the worst crashes of his career and sustained a severe concussion. He would rebound, though, and win a third and final championship with Johnson in 1985. This same year he would win the inaugural running of the Winston, NASCAR's all-star race.

Though he would go on to win more races with Hendrick Motorsports, including his only Daytona 500 victory, Waltrip would never repeat the success he enjoyed with Johnson.

On September 11, 1977 another new name appeared in the record book. Neil Bonnett was an Alabama native who had long been associated with Bobby Allison. When Allison's Winston Cup schedule became so demanding that he could not fulfill his obligations on the modified circuit, he had hired Bonnett. Along with Donnie Allison they formed a trio that was almost unbeatable in Sportsman competition, and earned the nickname "Alabama Gang". Indirectly, Allison paved the way for Bonnett's entrance into Winston Cup racing. When Allison, dismayed over a winless campaign in '76, suddenly quit the Roger Penske Matador team, he was replaced by Dave Marcis. This left a vacancy in Marcis' Dodge ,which was filled by Bonnett. Though abandoned by K & K Insurance, the teams long time sponsor, Bonnett and crew chief Harry Hyde persevered. Their initial victory at Richmond came at an average speed of 80.644 mph

His greatest period of success was during the early 1980's in the Wood brothers' famous number 21. He scored a total of nine victories in his first stint as the driver of this legendary machine. Throughout the eighties he would compete successfully for several teams, including a few years driving for Junior Johnson.

In 1990 Bonnett's career was suddenly put on hiatus. At the Spring race at Darlington Ernie Irvan set of a massive wreck and Bonnett was one of those involved. He was pulled from the car and walked away from the carnage unharmed. However, once at the hospital, it became clear that he didn't know who or where he was or how he came to be there. He was unable to smell or recognize food , and almost unbelievably, didn't recognize his wife,children,or parents. This hellish scenario played out for many weeks until finally Bonnett recalled a detail from a hunting trip with Dale Earnhardt. Other memories would return, but slowly. So slowly in fact that Bonnett could not return to the race track,and was forced to find other employment. He found it in the television broadcast booth where he was very well liked and where, sadly, he should have stayed.

The Elliott's were a racing family from Dawsonville, Georgia. The patriarch, George, used money from his junkyard and other businesses to finance a team manned by his three sons. Ernie built the engines while Dan was in charge of the body and chassis. In the cockpit was the third Elliott son, Bill.

After honing their skills on the local tracks in North Georgia, the trio began to field second hand Fords and Mercurys in the occasional Winston Cup event. They maintained a limited schedule and met with limited success through the late seventies.

Finally, the team was bought by Harry Melling in 1981 and

within two years the Elliotts were campaigning full time. Bill scored his first victory in the last race of 1983 on the road course at Riverside, California.

Elliott soared to unprecedented success in 1985 when he won three of NASCAR's four premier events to claim the first million dollar bonus payed out by R.J. Reynolds. This was a promotional event dreamed up by the late T. Wayne Robertson, a Reynolds employee. The idea was to focus on four distinctive races:the oldest,the longest,the fastest, and the most lucrative. Any driver that could win three of them would be entitled to a cool million dollar bonus. During one of these events at Talladega mechanical problems caused Elliott to go two laps down. Incredibly, he was able to erase the five mile deficit on the race track on his way to the win. His victory total for the year was eleven.

In 1987 he won the pole at Talladega by posting a speed of 212.809 mph, a record that most likely will never be broken. He put the final punctuation on his career in 1988 with his only championship.

In 1986, NASCAR's top division, which had been known as the Winston Cup Grand National division, had it's name changed to "The Winston Cup Series". NASCAR's Sportsman division would assume the name "Grand National", and would reach a sponsorship agreement with Busch beer.

Of course, the first race under the new banner was the "Daytona 500" on February 16, in which the winner was Geoff Bodine in a Chevrolet. It was his first and only victory in this event and probably the biggest win of his career. Bodine made one more trip to victory lane in '86, at a May race at Dover.

Several new faces appeared in the winner's circle in '86, though one of them had an all too familiar name. Kyle Petty was born June 2,1960, in Randleman,North Carolina. He followed his legendary father into racing, first appeared in a Winston Cup race in 1979, and ran his first full schedule in 1981. Unlike Richard, it would take Kyle seven years and a little luck to score his first victory. The second race of the season was on February 23 at Martinsville. On the next to last lap, Petty was half a lap off the pace set by Dale Earnhardt. Suddenly, Earnhardt and Darrelll Waltrip collided, and the ensuing crash disabled the top four machines. Petty steered through the debris to claim the yellow flag and his first career victory. This made him the first third generation driver to win at NASCAR's highest level.

More history would be made when the series moved to Talladega. On April 30,1987 Bill Elliott won the pole for the "Winston 500" with a speed of 212.809 mph. This was the fastest lap ever recorded by a stock car. Given the nature of the rules today, this record may never be broken. The 500 itself, on May 3, produced a new, although somewhat familiar, name for the record book. The race had to be halted ten miles early due to darkness. When this happened the driver who was declared the winner was Davey Allison. Allison, the son of NASCAR legend Bobby Allison, claimed his first victory in his #28 Ford.

This made the Allison's the third family to produce a second generation Winston Cup winner.

On June 14, 1987 Tim Richmond staged one the greatest comebacks that NASCAR has ever seen. Two weeks after his Riverside victory had ended the previous season, Richmond had been hospitalized near his parents home in Ohio. At the time the diagnosis was limited to extreme pneumonia. Richmond was so ill that he remained in the hospital for a month and missed the first eleven races of 1987. By June, however, he was back, driving his Chevrolet to victory at Pocono. To punctuate his feat, he also won the following week at Riverside. In a coincidence reminiscent of Joe Weatherly, this was Richmond's thirteenth victory and also his last.

NASCAR's experiment with restrictor plates in the '70's could be characterized as a success in that it eventually forced all the teams to switch to small block engines. However, engine builders and crew chiefs had been steadily gleaning more and more power from the smaller power plants. This culminated in Bill Elliott's mind boggling speed of 212 mph at Talladega in 1987. The same year and at the same track Bobby Allison was involved in a terrifying single car accident. As he sped through Talladega's front stretch, Allison's car became airborne at approximately 210 m.p.h. It barrel rolled along the catch fence and through some miracle did not fly into the crowd. NASCAR felt that it had to intervene again, and plates were reinstated in 1988 at Daytona and Talladega, where they are still in place today.

Whether or not plates were a factor, the 1988 edition of the "Daytona 500" was one of the most memorable ever. Absent from the field which took the green flag on Valentine's Day was Tim Richmond. NASCAR had become concerned that Richmond was plagued by more than just pneumonia and insisted on seeing his medical records. Richmond refused and was denied a medical clearance to race. About an hour after the start of the 500, a small plane appeared over the speedway. It was towing a banner which bore this message: "Fans,I Miss You, Tim Richmond". The banner would appear on the CBS telecast of the event.

Then, just after the halfway point of the race, came one of the most horrific crashes in Daytona's history. As he drove through the tri-oval in the front stretch, Richard Petty was tapped from behind by Phil Barkdoll. Petty's car spun completely around then became airborne. Spinning on it's nose, the car rolled five times along the retaining fence, dropped to the track where it rolled seven times, then finally flipped end over end twice. The car eventually came to a rest, only to be struck by the cars of Brett Bodine and A.J. Foyt. Amazingly, Petty survived with relatively minor injuries.

Though this should have been plenty, more excitement was in store for the 135,000 fans who were present. On the final lap the leader was Bobby Allison, with his son Davey close behind. As they left turn four, Davey moved to his father's inside but was unable to make the pass. Bobby Allison had won his third "Daytona 500" at the age of 50. This was the first time a father and son duo had finished first and second since Lee and Richard Petty had done so in a rain shortened race at Heidelberg Stadium, near Pittsburgh, in 1960. Though no one would have guessed it at the time, it was also Bobby Allison's last win.

The summer of 1988 brought the third, after Lake Speed and Phil Parsons, of four new winners in the Winston Cup season. Ken Schrader was born on May 29,1955, in Fenton,Missouri. As a Mid-Westerner, Schrader came up through the USAC ranks, winning Dirt Car and Sprint Car national championships. He first appeared in a Winston Cup race in 1984, driving a Ford owned by Elmo Langley. In 1988 he moved to the second Chevrolet owned by Rick Hendrick. The move soon paid off, as Schrader won the "Talladega-DieHard 500" on July 31. The fourth new winner in 1988 was Alan Kulwicki. Kulwicki was a Wisconsin native and one of the few driver-owners on the circuit. Fittingly, his first victory came at a new track for NASCAR. Phoenix International Raceway is a one mile track in Phoenix, Arizona. It was built in 1964, and the banking in the paved oval does not exceed 11 degrees. Kulwicki's win, on November 6, came in the first top level NASCAR race held in Arizona since 1960.

The new face in victory lane in 1989 belonged to Mark

Martin. Martin, a native of Batesville, Arkansas, was born on January 9,1959. Competing on some of the same Mid-Western tracks that had spawned Rusty Wallace and Ken Schrader, Martin was a four time ASA champion. He first appeared on the circuit in 1981, ran a full schedule the following year, but by 1987 appeared in only one event. In 1988, he joined a new teamed owned by a drag racer turned businessman named Jack Roush, and ran a full schedule once again In '89, his initial victory came at Rockingham on October 22. In the intervening years Martin has proved to be adept at every size and shape of track. He has enjoyed so much success that it is almost unbelievable that he has never won a championship. He scored one of the most famous second place finishes in NASCAR history when a suspect carburetor caused the sanctioning body to deduct points from him after a race at Richmond. The move was controversial and Martin eventually lost the title to Dale Earnhardt by the slimmest of margins.

Some of the most interesting developments in the 1994 Winston Cup campaign took place during the off-season as well as off the track. One of these was the most significant safety modification in years. The wedge-like shape of a Winston Cup car, and it's rear spoiler, are designed to force the vehicle downwards. When a car is turned backwards , the opposite effect is achieved as the car becomes what is essentially a wing. This could result in horrific crashes, such as those which Rusty Wallace had suffered the previous year at Daytona and Talladega. NASCAR's solution to this problem, which it mandated for all cars in '94, was "roof flaps". Roof flaps are rectangular sheets of metal in the top of the car. When a car is turned backwards the airflow over the roof lifts the flaps into an upright position. This disrupts the airflow, prevents "lift" from developing, and usually keeps the car on the ground.

The other new wrinkle for '94 was another tire war. Hoosier Racing Tire has announced a return to Winston Cup competition, directly challenging Goodyear. Those who felt that a tire war compromised safety soon had evidence that they were correct.

While Dale Earnhardt had notched his first championship with owner Rod Osterlund in 1980, it would not be until the late Eighties and the Nineties that he made a run at the history books. It started in 1986 ,which was Tim Richmond's most successful campaign. It was not enough to deliver him a championship,however. That distinction went, for the second time, to Earnhardt. Earnhardt had gone to victory lane at Darlington, North Wilkesboro, Atlanta, and twice at Charlotte. He had racked up 4,468 points on the strength of 23 top ten finishes. The rest of the top ten were Darrell Waltrip, Richmond, Bill Elliott, Ricky Rudd, Rusty Wallace, Bobby Allison, Geoff Bodine, Bobby Hillin,Jr., and Kyle Petty. Three of these drivers, Earnhardt, Waltrip, and Elliott, surpassed $1 million in earnings.

In 1987, Dale Earnhardt would defend his title with the most dominant campaign of his career. On March 1 he embarked on a rampage which was perhaps the most prodigious of his career. Of the next seven races, Earnhardt claimed the checkered flag at six. His wins came at Rockingham, Richmond, Darlington, North Wilkesboro, Bristol, and Martinsville.

In the second half of the season Bill Elliott did his utmost to flummox Earnhardt. The challenge came in the form of wins at Talladega, Michigan, Charlotte, and Rockingham. Earnhardt responded, however, with victories at Pocono, Bristol, and Richmond. He also won his first "Southern 500" in a rain shortened race at Darlington.

Elliott won the season's final race, which was now at Atlanta rather than Riverside, on November 22. It was , however, too little, too late. Earnhardt became the sixth driver to win three titles with 4,696 points, more than 400 ahead of second place Elliott. Earnhardt also became the second driver to surpass $2 million in winnings for a single season. The rest of the top ten were Terry Labonte, Darrell Waltrip, Rusty Wallace, Ricky Rudd, Kyle Petty, Richard Petty, and Bobby Allison.

The 1990 Winston Cup season, which would end with history being made, began with something of a fluke. Though his resume was nothing if not impressive, one plateau Earnhardt had not reached was a victory in the "Daytona 500". He seemed poised to change that on February 18,1990, in the 32nd running of the storied event. Earnhardt started on the front row, alongside Ken Schrader, who was now driving Junior Johnson's #11 Chevrolet. It was the #3 Chevrolet of Earnhardt, however, that dominated from the start. With a lead that sometimes stretched to 39 seconds, Earnhardt led 155 of the 200 laps. However, fate soon dictated that he would not lead the final lap. As he cruised down the backstretch to a certain checkered flag, Earnhardt's right rear tire was cut by a piece of debris on the track. The tire flattened through the final turns, causing the car to fishtail and slide towards the outside wall. This cleared the way for the second place driver, Derrike Cope, to charge to the finish line and his first Winston Cup win.

Though this was probably the greatest disappointments of his career, Earnhardt quickly rebounded. He won the fourth and fifth races of the year, which came at Atlanta and Darlington. This second victory was a bittersweet one. It was in this race that one of his closest friends, Neil Bonnett, suffered near fatal injuries. Bonnett later related that after his release from the hospital he could not recognize his wife and children. When he was fully recovered, Bonnett climbed not into the driver's seat, but into the television announcer's booth.

Earnhardt went on to win races at Talladega and Michigan. He then closed out the first half of the season by winning the "Pepsi 400" on July 7.The cumulative results of Earnhardt's campaign turned out to be his greatest accomplishment in 1990. With 4,430 points, he became only the second driver to win as many as four championships. Also, on the strength of his nine wins, he became the first driver in motor sports history to surpass $3 million in winnings for a single season.

The field that challenged Earnhardt for his title in 1991 was a crowded one, as fourteen different drivers claimed a checkered flag. Among them were a first time winner and a veteran having his greatest year.

In the "Daytona 500" on February 17, Erinie Irvan proved that he was no flash in the pan by claiming NASCAR's most famous event as his second win. He was also beginning to earn the ire of other drivers, along with the nickname "Swervin' Irvan", with a driving style that some felt was too aggressive.

Dale Earnhardt would claim two short track victories in the first half of the season. These wins came at Richmond and Martinsville.

As the season wound down, Earnhardt collected one more win and Davey Allison scored two, before Mark Martin won the final race of the year at Atlanta on November 17. Things had changed in NASCAR so much that Dale Earnhardt now represented the old guard. This was evidenced by the fact only Richard Petty could claim more championships. Though Harry Gant and Allison had more victories in '91, Earnhardt won his fifth title with relative ease, his 4,287 points placing him almost 200 ahead of Ricky Rudd. The rest of the top ten were Allison, Gant, Ernie Irvan, Mark Martin, Sterling Marlin, Darrell Waltrip, Ken Schrader, and Rusty Wallace. Incredibly, each of the top six had surpassed $1 million in earnings.

The 1993 Cup Season should have been an epic battle as Rusty Wallace won ten races, including the final race of the year was at Atlanta on November 14. However, Wallace had also failed to finish a number of races, notably at Daytona and Talladega where he suffered spectacular crashes. This enabled Dale Earnhardt to claim an incredible sixth title with 4,526 points. He also surpassed $3 million in winnings for the second time in his career.

The 1994 season started as a duel between Rusty Wallace and Erni Irvan. As if to remind these two drivers that he was still the champion, Dale Earnhardt claimed the checkered flag at three of five Spring races. His victories came at Darlington, Bristol, and Talladega.

In September, Rusty Wallace tried to mount a challenge to points leader Earnhardt as he won races at Dover and Martinsville. However, in both cases Earnhardt finished right behind him. Given that Earnhardt clinched the title on October 23 at Rockingham, the '94 points race could only described as boring. The exciting part was that Earnhardt had won an incredible seventh championship, tying him with Richard Petty. With his team seemingly in at it's peak, a record breaking eighth title seemed almost guaranteed. Sadly, it was not to be.

Without a doubt the most meteoric figure in stock car racing in the last quarter century has been Jeff Gordon. He was born in Vallejo,California in 1971 and was racing go-carts at a very early age. When he reached his teens his stepfather moved the family to Indiana specifically to advance the young man's racing career.

During this period Gordon competed in quarter midget and midget cars in USAC sponsored events. He was overwhelmingly dominant in these series, racking up over 500 wins. By the age of eighteen he faced a problem many of us would like to have: too many opportunities.

Using average length of a career, length of a season, and total prize money available, Gordon was able to calculate that NASCAR held the most promise for him.

Competing in the Busch series he performed just as many had expected, garnering Rookie of the Year status in 1991 and three victories in 1992. In the final race of 1992 Gordon made his Winston Cup debut at Atlanta. This was famously and perhaps symbolically also the last race for Richard Petty.

His first full year was 1993 and to the surprise of no one he was Rookie of the Year. 1994 would see him score his first win in the 600 at Charlotte. Later that summer he won NASCAR's first race at the Indianapolis Motor Speedway. This was a huge event and Gordon was soon exhibiting a knack for winning on the biggest stages.

He was the Winston Cup champion in 1995 and since then has amassed three more titles and millions of dollars in winnings. Perhaps more importantly,however, is that he has totally remade the landscape of the sport. NASCAR's push into new geographic territory and new television contracts would almost certainly have been less successful without him. He pushed the amount that a top tier team could demand from a sponsor to new levels. The overnight search for the next Jeff Gordon resulted in younger and younger drivers from more diverse areas. A Winston Cup race today routinely features more drivers from California, Washington,Oregon, and Indiana than from the Southeast.

Though the competition has caught up to him, and Gordon is certainly not done with his assault on the record book, the mark his early years left on the sport is indelible.

One of NASCAR's least likely competitors and champions was Wisconsin native Alan Kulwicki. The brainy inventor of several devices used in racing, he was born in 1954 and began

162

his career as a teenager on the local tracks of his home state. By the early eighties he was competing in ASA and USAC, where his father had once been an engine builder.

By 1985 Kulwicki had moved to Charlotte to wage his first full time Winston Cup campaign. Though he finished with Rookie of the Year honors, it would not be until 1988 that he would find victory lane at Phoenix. He celebrated this feat by making a clockwise circuit of the track, which was dubbed a "Polish victory lap." He was offered the chance to drive for Junior Johnson in 1990 but preferred to keep battling in his own single car team.

In 1992 Kulwicki accomplished something that is simply unimaginable today. Still competing as an independent owner\driver,he captured victories at both Pocono races as well as one at Bristol. When the series reached it's last race at Atlanta, he was locked in a battle for the title with Bill Elliott and Davey Allison. Allison suffered an early setback which left only Kulwicki and Elliott competing for the championship. The late stages of the race were caution free, but as every one else pitted for fuel Kulwicki stayed on the track, pressing his luck to it's very limits. Elliott would win the race, but Kulwicki's gamble meant that he had led 103 laps, one more than Elliott. This resulted in Kulwicki being awarded the standard 10 point bonus for leading the most laps. This same 10 points would be his margin of victory for the championship. This remains one of the closest and most exciting points battles in NASCAR's history.

In 2004 NASCAR introduced a new format for crowning a

champion, called the Chase for the Cup. Competitors would race for points as before until the final ten races of the season. At this point the top ten drivers would have their points reset and would enter the Chase, in which each was eligible to win the title. This made for some mid-season excitement as those drivers just above and below the cutoff point waged a battle to see who would be in and who would be out. The number of drivers in the Chase was later expanded to twelve. Though the format has not been quite as exciting as hoped, most years the question of who will be champion has come down to the final race.

2004 also marked the end of NASCAR's longtime association with R.J. Reynolds, which meant that it's premier series would no longer bear the name Winston Cup. Instead, a sponsorship deal was reached with cell phone provider Nextel, which resulted in a name change to the Nextel Cup Series. Nextel would later be acquired by Sprint and the name would change again to the Sprint Cup Series.

In 2007 Toyota teams began to compete full time in Nextel Cup races. This marked the first time that a foreign make of car had competed in NASCAR's top division since the 1950's. The first teams were owned by Michael Waltrip, Bill Davis, and Red Bull, a European energy drink. They were soon joined by Joe Gibbs Racing, which provided Toyota with it's first victory when Kyle Busch drove to victory lane at Atlanta on March 10,2008.

Also in 2007, the trend of open wheeled racers competing on the NASCAR circuit hit full steam. It all started in 1999 when Tony Stuart came to NASCAR and took Rookie of the Year honors. Young drivers such as Kasey Kahne and Ryan Newman soon followed. Still later, champions from other series such as Sam Hornish,Jr. and Juan Pablo Montoya made the move to NASCAR. Even Indy darling Danica Patrick couldn't resist, running a limited schedule in the Nationwide series for Dale Earnhardt, Jr. in 2010. None of these drivers,however, have had near the success as Stewart, who to date has earned two Cup championships.

Another big development in 2007 was the unveiling of the Car of Tomorrow. This was a common body design that would be used for all makes in Sprint Cup competition. The only differences between a Ford, Chevy, Dodge, or Toyota would now be found only under the hood. The COT body featured a horizontal splitter on the front valence and a raised wing on the rear deck. It's most important features, however, were not so obvious. The COT had it's genesis in the wake of Dale Earnhardt's death, so while reduced costs were part of it's appeal, increased safety was it's primary impetus. In the new design the driver's seat was moved away from the door and the roll cage was shifted to the rear and had increased head room. Also, energy absorbing baffles were added to the side panels.

The COT was an instant success, so much so that it's first full campaign was moved up a year from 2009 to 2008.

In 2009 Frank Kimmel would tie Iggy Katona's record of six ARCA championships.

Jeff Gordon's rise to prominence precipitated an influx of new, young drivers into NASCAR. All of this talent eventually rose to meet the new standard that Gordon had set. By the early 2000's NASCAR had achieved a kind of parity. Gone were the days when only four or five drivers had any chance of finding victory lane. Instead, fully half the field were previous winners and were driving cars that had every chance of taking the checkered flag.

However, by the second half of the century's first decade, one driver and one team threatened to annihilate the balance that had been established. The team, interestingly enough, was originally part owned by Jeff Gordon. The driver was Jimmie Johnson.

Johnson was born on September 17,1975 in El Cajon, California. He began his racing career on motorcycles at the tender age of five. He then moved to off-road racing, scoring championships and Rookie of the Year honors in several different series. By the late 1990's he was competing in the ASA and NASCAR's Busch series. While driving for Herzog Motorsports during this period he met two men who would prove instrumental to his career: Jeff Gordon and Chad Knaus. Through several full years on the Busch circuit he would win only a single race.

It was as though he flipped a switch, however, in 2002, his first full season at NASCAR's top level. He scored three victories and was fifth in the points race, but amazingly failed to win Rookie of the Year. In 2003 he began to show a penchant for the big stage. He won both the Winston and the 600 at Lowe's Motor Speedway in Charlotte, no doubt to the delight of his primary sponsor, Lowe's Home Improvement. He also vaulted to second in the points battle behind Matt Kenseth. Over the next two years he would collect twelve wins, including the 600 again, as well as the Southern 500, and would finish in the top ten in both campaigns.

It was in 2006 that Johnson and Knaus began to rewrite the record book in earnest. In '06 Johnson won the Daytona 500 and the Brickyard 400 on his way to racking up his first championship. He then dominated NASCAR's top series, which had been renamed the Nextel Cup Series, on his way to a second title in 2007. He won at the Brickyard again in 2008, but more impressively he won his third consecutive title. Cale Yarborough had been the only driver to do so previously. Yarborough's record had stood for decades and many presumed that it was unassailable.

In 2009 Johnson won at Indy and Daytona again and scored a record breaking fourth championship. He became only the fourth driver to win as many titles and the first to win four in a row. In 2010 it appeared as though the rest of the field may have caught up with Johnson and Knaus. Kevin Harvick and Denny Hamlin clearly had the two best cars and were at the top of the points battle for virtually the entire season. However, when the checkered flag fell at the final race at Homestead

Speedway, Johnson was within striking distance of the title. Harvick and Hamlin both suffered missteps during the race, but Johnson started in fifth place and remained steady all day, eventually finishing second and claiming a fifth title. He became only the third driver to win as many titles, eclipsing his car owner and mentor, Jeff Gordon. He is also approaching the territory that has been preserved for only Richard Petty and Dale Earnhardt. Any conversation about the all time greatest stock car racers must include Jimmie Johnson.

In January of 2011 NASCAR announced that it would revamp it's points system in the Sprint Cup series for the first time in decades. Under the new plan the first place driver would receive 43 points. Each successive finisher would receive one less point with the last place driver getting one point. In addition, a three point bonus would be awarded for the win, along with one point bonuses for leading a lap and leading the most laps. The maximum points a driver could score would be 48.

Also, changes were made to the Chase format. For the 2011 season the ten drivers with the most points would enter the Chase for the championship. They would be joined by the two drivers between 11th and 20th position with the most wins. As in past years, this would make a total of twelve drivers who enter the Chase and are eligible for the title.

The Men Behind The Machines Part4

The Wood Brothers are, with the possible exception of the Petty's, the most famous stock car racing team in the sport's history. Beginning in the mid-1950's and with all five brothers initially involved, the team would be distilled to just Glen and Leonard Wood by the late 50's. Though Glen did some racing and had some success, even in the early days the brothers preferred to hire an outside driver.

Early successes came with drivers Speedy Thompson, Curtis Turner, and "Fireball" Roberts behind the wheel. By the 60's the team was renowned for it's engines and chassis, and they were famously hired as a pit crew for the 1965 Indy 500. The Wood's stellar performance helped Jim Clark to the victory.

It was in the 70's, mostly with David Pearson, that the team enjoyed it's greatest success. Running a limited super speedway schedule, they won 46 out of 143 races entered in just seven years. In 1976, the year of Pearson's sensational win in the

Daytona 500, they also won the 600 at Charlotte and the Southern 500 at Darlington.

In later years well known names such as Davey Allison, Dale Jarrett, Kyle Petty, Michael Waltrip, Morgan Shepard, Eliot Sadler, and Bill Elliot would pilot the famous #21, but success would fall off significantly from their prime years.

While some families produce second generation drivers, the Woods produced second generation owners. Today the team is run by Eddie and Len Wood and is the oldest continuously operating team in NASCAR. It was under the younger Wood's leadership that the team returned to form in a stunning victory at the 2011 Daytona 500 with driver Trevor Bayne behind the wheel.

Harry Hyde was born on January 17,1925 in Brownsville,Kentucky. Like many others,he developed his skills as a mechanic during World War II. He slowly built his reputation as a driver and more importantly as a car builder throughout the Mid-West over the next two decades.

In 1965 he was hired as the crew chief for the K&K Insurance Dodge, eventually teaming with Bobby Isaac for his greatest success and his sole championship in 1970. In the early eighties Hyde was a partner of Rick Hendrick in a new race team, but was eventually bought out by Hendrick. He was later rehired as a crew chief and had considerable success with drivers Tim Richmond and Ken Schrader. He parted ways with Hendrick for good in the early '90's and though he continued to work on the Winston Cup circuit it was on teams that were seldom competitive.

Hyde died in 1996 but left behind a very impressive legacy of 56 wins and 88 poles.

Jake Elder was born in 1936 and got his start as a fabricator for Petty Enterprises in the 1960's. By the late '60's he had worked his way up to crew chief for Holman-Moody where he won championships in 1968 and '69 with David Pearson behind the wheel. He worked with a myriad of teams throughout the Seventies, earning the nickname "Suitcase Jake". Two drivers whom he guided to their first victories were Darrell Waltrip and Dale Earnhardt. He was also crew chief for Earnhardt for the first portion of 1980, which was Earnhardt's first championship season.

Ray Evernham was born in 1957 in Hazlet, New Jersey. He raced Modifieds in his early years, but his technical ability, especially in the area of chassis adjustments, soon found him behind the wall. In 1990 he worked on a few chassis for an up and coming driver named Jeff Gordon. When a position became available on Gordon's team at Bill Davis Racing a few years later, Evernham was tapped to fill it. However, Ford had to foot the bill for his salary because Bill Davis was not as enthralled with Evernham as Gordon was.

By 1994 Evernham and Gordon would graduate to Winston Cup and Rick Hendrick Motorsports. Jack Rousch had been pursuing Gordon as well, but Gordon wanted to bring Evernham with him and Roush balked at the idea of not picking the crew chief himself. Hendrick had no such qualms and gladly brought both Gordon and Evernham into the fold. Together they would launch Gordon's assault on the record books, notching 47 wins and three championships before parting ways.

In 1999 Evernham formed his own team and was instrumental in Dodge's return to NASCAR after a fifteen year absence. He would score wins with Jeremy Mayfield and Bill Elliott and eventually meld the team with Richard Petty Motorsports. This new, larger team would find the winner's circle again with Kasey Kahne behind the wheel in 2009.

Naturally gifted and with a technical education,Robert Yates' ability to coax horsepower out of an engine caused him to be an in demand crew member beginning in the mid-Seventies. He built the power plants for such champion drivers as Cale Yarborough, Darrell Waltrip, and Bobby Allison.

In 1988 he purchased the team owned by Harry Rainier and J.T. Lundy, which came complete with a young driver named Davey Allison. Allison would eventually score 15 wins for the team before his tragic helicopter crash in 1993. Yates would soldier on, and eventually return to the winner's circle with Ernie Irvan and Dale Jarrett behind the wheel.

End of the Road

The 1951 Grand National season closed with a race at Lakeview Speedway in Mobile, Alabama on November 25. The winner, back in his Studebaker, was Frank Mundy. This was the last Grand National race ever won by a Studebaker.

The last Daytona beach race was run in 1958. It was won by Frank Mundy who outran Curtis Turner on his way to the checkered flag.

In the early Seventies Fred Lorenzen would stage an ill-fated comeback. He raced in the 600 at Charlotte in 1970 and other key events but results were mediocre at best. At the 1971 Southern 500 he had an opportunity to drive a Mercury Cyclone for the Wood Brothers. During practice for the event he was producing phenomenal lap times but lost control of the machine in turn four. The car struck the outside retaining wall then zoomed across the track and hit the pit wall. The ensuing crash was horrific, as the Mercury became airborne and struck several light poles before the disintegrated, flaming mess came to a stop. Lorenzen's last start in a Cup race would come in 1972 at Martinsville.

On October 10,1971 the last race was run at Langhorne Speedway. In this 200 mile event for modifieds the winner was Roger Treichler. This truly legendary track fell victim to the bulldozer just days later.

After just over a decade of hosting Cup races, the Texas World Speedway appeared on the Cup schedule for the last time on June 7, 1981. The winner, with a last lap pass of Dale Earnhardt, was Benny Parsons.

A race of note came in 1988. On June 12, Rusty Wallace drove his Pontiac to victory lane in a 400 kilometer race at Riverside. This was the last NASCAR race run on the California road course which had first appeared on the schedule in 1958.

On June 19,1988 the "Miller High Life 500" produced a near fatal tragedy for Bobby Allison. Allison, whose Buick was sponsored by Miller, had his right rear tire go flat on the first lap. The car spun and slid sideways down the track. It was then clipped by the car of Jimmy Means and spun again. This left the car sideways on the track , with the driver's side facing the oncoming traffic. Allison was then T-boned by the Chevrolet of Chauncey "Jocko" Maggiocomo. Both drivers sustained major injuries. Allison, who has never been able to recall the accident, spent almost four months in the hospital. It was the last time he would appear in a Winston Cup race.

Richard Petty's last win played out as though it had been scripted by a Hollywood screenwriter. It occurred on the Fourth of July in 1984 on a track with which Petty had made himself synonymous:the Daytona International Speedway.

The race was lent a special aura even before it began by it's Grand Marshall, President Ronald Reagan, who gave the command to fire engines from mid-air. Photographers would later capture stunning images of Petty's famed #43 streaking down the backstretch as Air Force One landed in the background on the runway adjacent to the speedway.

On lap 158 Doug Heveron wrecked, leaving Petty and Cale Yarborough to race back to the caution flag. Petty edged Yarborough by a fender to claim his seventh and final 500. It was also his 200th and last win in NASCAR's elite division.

Petty was later congratulated by President Reagan as the pair exchanged niceties before the TV cameras. There they were, the King and the Gipper, two earnest men who rose to the pinnacle of their professions by adhering to simple principles. Do they even make them like that anymore?

The last Cup race at North Wilkesboro was on September 29,1996, and was won by Jeff Gordon. After founder Enoch Staley died in 1995 it became clear that NASCAR had only continued to race at this small market track out of loyalty to him. The half stake in the track not owned by the Staley family was bought by Bruton Smith and Speedway Motorsports. To keep Smith from gaining complete ownership the Staleys sold their half to Bob Bahre. The tracks two dates were then moved to the brand new Texas Motorspeedway and the New Hampshire Motor Speedway.

After almost four decades as a mainstay on the circuit, the last Cup race at Rockingham was run on February 22,2004. Like North Wilkesboro, the small market track was bought by large corporate interest so it's race dates could be moved to larger, more lucrative venues.

10225871R0

Made in the USA
Lexington, KY
05 July 2011